Oscar Wilde's

The IMPORTANCE of Being EARNEST

A new approach for a new course

Annotations, analysis and activities by
Eoghan Evesson

educate.ie

PUBLISHED BY:
Educate.ie
Walsh Educational Books Ltd
Castleisland, Co. Kerry, Ireland
www.educate.ie

EDITOR:
Julie Steenson

DESIGN & LAYOUT:
Kieran O'Donoghue

COVER DESIGN:
Kieran O'Donoghue

PRINTED AND BOUND BY:
Walsh Colour Print, Castleisland

PHOTOGRAPHS:

Front cover photograph: Javelin Films

AF archive/Alamy; Bigstock; Ealing Studios; Elliott Franks/ArenaPAL; Javelin Films; KINGWILL Marilyn/ArenaPAL; NORRINGTON Nigel/ArenaPAL; Ronald Grant Archive (RGA); Smock Alley Theatre/Tom Maher (photographer)/Clodagh Mooney Duggan as Gwendolen Fairfax; Smock Alley Theatre/Tom Maher (photographer)/James Murphy as Jack Worthing, Clodagh Mooney Duggan as Gwendolen Fairfax; Smock Alley Theatre/Tom Maher (photographer)/Katie McCann as Miss Prism; TOPFOTO/ArenaPAL; UNIVERSITY OF BRISTOL/ArenaPAL; ©UPPA/TopFoto; Wikimedia Commons

ILLUSTRATIONS:
Bigstock

ISBN: 978-1-910468-68-5

Dedication

To my wife Sharon, for all that you've given and for keeping me earnest.

Acknowledgements

Our children Beth, Alex and Susie. Susan, Thomas, Betty, Mick and all my family. Paul Meany and Pat O'Mahony for getting me started. Matt O'Shea and POB for keeping me going. All the wonderful parents, staff, pupils and teachers of Newbridge College. Special thanks to Sinéad and Julie at Educate.ie for making this book happen.

Eoghan Evesson

CONTENTS

Teacher's Introduction

As part of the new Junior Cycle English Specification, a prescribed list of texts was published by the NCCA for pupils studying Junior Cycle English until June 2019. Pupils studying under the new specification are asked to study a variety of dramatic texts in First Year and are required to study **two** dramatic texts (one of which can be studied in extract form) in Second and Third Year.

To this end, a welcome addition to the prescribed list was Oscar Wilde's *The Importance of Being Earnest*. By studying this edition of the play, and using the accompanying portfolio, pupils will be engaged with all **39 learning outcomes** and the **seven statements of learning** (relating to English) that have been created within the new Junior Cycle English framework.

To aid learning, the three acts of the play have been divided into manageable parts. Each part ends with a bank of activities and exercises, many of which are intended to be recorded in the portfolio. It is not expected that every task will be completed by a class group. Indeed, it is hoped that enough options have been provided so that teachers will be able to pick and choose the tasks that suit their particular group.

The Portfolio

The tasks in the portfolio have also been developed to encourage pupil development across the **eight key skills** in the Junior Cycle framework:

- Being numerate
- Managing information and thinking
- Staying well
- Managing myself

- Being literate
- Communicating
- Working with others
- Being creative

At the end of each act, pupils are asked to reflect on their learning through project work. These projects have been created to help pupils prepare for the **Oral Communication** and **Collection of Texts** tasks that they will have to complete during Second and Third Year. Many of these projects can be completed by mixing different elements of the task, resulting in over a dozen possible projects. The portfolio includes a blank **student reflection note** for each project.

The portfolio also includes a **character file**, a **mapping the plot** section and **end-of-act word searches** to help students consolidate their learning when they reach certain points in the play.

The portfolio is designed as a place for pupils to collect and log their learning as they move through the play.

Student's Introduction

About the Play

The Importance of Being Earnest was first performed on 14 February (Valentine's Day) 1895 at St James's Theatre in London.

Structure

The play is divided into **three acts**.

St James's Theatre

- **Act 1** introduces the characters and central **conflicts** in the play (the use of false identities and the challenges the characters must overcome to achieve love and marriage).
- **Act 2** shows how these conflicts play out and come to a head.
- **Act 3** shows how these conflicts are resolved.

Note: in this edition of the play, the three acts have been divided into shorter parts. This will help you to think about what happens in each act in more detail. However, *when you are writing about the play for assessment, it is important that you reference Acts 1, 2 and 3 only*, rather than the parts.

Genre

The Importance of Being Earnest is a **comedy**. There are a number of different types of comedy in the play.

Romantic comedy	Romantic comedy deals with love in a light way and revolves around the obstacles that a couple must overcome to find happiness. *The Importance of Being Earnest* follows the problems faced by two main couples, Jack and Gwendolen, and Algernon and Cecily.
Comedy of manners	This type of comedy uses **satire** to comment on society. It does this by making fun of common beliefs, attitudes and behaviours. The snobbish views of upper-class Victorian society are satirised by Wilde throughout the play.
Farce	This type of comedy entertains its audience with over-the-top characters and highly unlikely events. As you read *The Importance of Being Earnest*, you may find yourself thinking, 'That could never happen!' Wilde did this on purpose.

Although he was poking fun at Victorian society, the range of Wilde's comedy makes *The Importance of Being Earnest* as funny and sharp today as it was when it was written. It remains one of most performed plays in the world.

About the Author

Oscar Wilde was born in Dublin on 16 October 1854. Wilde studied classics (Latin and Greek literature, philosophy and history) at Trinity College Dublin, before going to Oxford University in England for further study. Later, he went to London, where he moved in fashionable circles and became one of the most well-known and respected writers of the time.

During his lifetime, Wilde wrote many essays, stories and poems, and one novel, *The Picture of Dorian Gray*. Wilde was best known for his comedy plays: *Lady Windermere's Fan* (1892), *A Woman of No Importance* (1893), *An Ideal Husband* (1895) and *The Importance of Being Earnest* (1895).

The Importance of Earnest was Wilde's last play. On the play's opening night, Wilde refused to come out and take a bow. Earlier that day, he had learned that John Douglas, the Marquess of Queensberry, planned to present him with rotten vegetables instead of the usual flowers at the curtain close. Queensberry had accused Wilde of being in a relationship with his son, Lord Alfred Douglas. When evidence of the relationship did appear, Wilde was arrested and put in prison for homosexuality.

Oscar Wilde

When Wilde was released from prison, he went to live in Paris. He died in Paris on 30 November 1900, aged 46.

Statue of Wilde in Merrion Square, Dublin

About the Victorian Period

The Victorian era of British history was the time when Queen Victoria was on the throne, from 1837 until her death in 1901.

There was a clear **class system** in place and there was a huge divide between the upper and lower classes.

The Victorians were known for their **strict morals** and the importance they put on **social conduct**. This meant that they had strong feelings about right and wrong and how people should behave.

Queen Victoria

Theme Tracker

Oscar Wilde had many themes and ideas in mind when he was writing *The Importance of Being Earnest*. The play's main themes are:

- Identity
- Love and marriage
- Social class
- Secrets and lies

As you read through the play, you will see icons beside lines of dialogue. These icons point out moments when one of the key themes is being shown. They will help you to keep the main themes in mind as you read the play. They will also help you to find quotes and examples when you come to write about the play's themes.

Theme Key

 Identity

 Love and marriage

 Social class

 Secrets and lies

Your Portfolio

As you study *The Importance of Being Earnest*, you will complete tasks in your portfolio. These tasks will help you to think about the play's **characters**, **themes** and **language** in more detail.

 **= portfolio time**

As you work through your portfolio, the **ACE system** will help you to approach tasks in a planned way, to complete them to the best of your ability and to identify where there might be room for improvement.

ACE stands for:

1. **A**nalyse (Plan)   2. **C**reate   3. **E**dit

You will find more information about how to use ACE in your task work on **page 3** of your portfolio.

At the end of each act, you can use your portfolio to complete a project. This project can help you to prepare for the Oral Communication and Collection of Texts tasks that you will carry out during Second and Third Year. Your portfolio includes ACE templates to help you complete these end-of-act projects. The portfolio also includes blank student reflection notes, which you should fill in once you have finished each project.

The portfolio also includes a **character file**, a **mapping the plot** section and **end-of-act word searches** to help you review what you have learned at the end of each act.

Glossary of Important Terms

ASIDE
A remark made by a character that the other characters on stage are not supposed to be able to hear but that the audience can hear. For example, during Gwendolen and Cecily's argument in Act 2, Gwendolen calls Cecily 'Detestable girl!' in an aside.

CLASSICAL ALLUSION
A reference to events or characters from Greek or Roman myth. Wilde studied classics at university, so he often makes these references in his writing. For example, in Act 1 Jack refers to Lady Bracknell as a 'Gorgon', a creature from Greek myth that has snakes for hair.

DRAMATIC IRONY
When the audience or characters on stage know something that other characters do not know. *The Importance of Being Earnest* relies on dramatic irony for much of its comedy. For example, in Act 1 the audience sees Algernon eating the cucumber sandwiches, then lying to Lady Bracknell about what happened to them.

EPIGRAM
An epigram is a short statement that is easily quoted. It is usually clever or witty. Wilde is the master of the epigram. For example, 'The truth is rarely pure and never simple', a line spoken by Algernon in *The Importance of Being Earnest*, is still widely quoted today.

EUPHEMISM
A mild or polite word or term that is used to say something harsh or embarrassing. For example, in Act 2 Cecily describes Gwendolen's engagement to Ernest as an 'unfortunate entanglement' as she does not wish to insult Gwendolen.

FOIL
A character whose actions and personality are used to highlight another character's behaviour by contrast. For example, servant Lane's calm and dutiful conduct is in contrast with his master Algernon's careless behaviour.

FORESHADOWING
A literary device (a method used by writers) used to hint at events that are yet to come in a text. There is a lot of foreshadowing in *The Importance of Being Earnest*. For example, at the start of Act 2 Miss Prism mentions that she wrote a novel in her youth. This novel will play an important role at the end of the play.

HYPERBOLE
Using exaggerated, over-the-top language for dramatic effect. Wilde uses hyperbole to create funny moments. For example, in Act 3 of *The Importance of Being Earnest* Cecily calls baptism a 'fearful ordeal'.

MOTIF
A repeated idea or object in a book or play that helps to develop its themes. One of the important motifs in *The Importance of Being Earnest* is the significance of names.

PUN
A play on words that sound the same but have different meanings. Puns provide comedy, but they can also add double meaning to what characters are saying. *The Importance of Being Earnest* plays on the fact that the name Ernest sounds exactly the same as the word 'earnest', which means being sincere or serious.

SOLILOQUY
A speech made by a character who is alone on stage. This allows the character to share their thoughts with the audience. For example, Algernon has two soliloquies in the play. In the first, he reveals what he thinks of the lower classes; in the second, he makes his love for Cecily known.

SYMBOL
An object, person or situation that represents (stands for) something else. Symbols are another way for a writer to explore an idea. In *The Importance of Being Earnest* food symbolises the greed and self-indulgence of the upper classes.

Oscar Wilde's

The Importance of Being EARNEST

A Trivial Comedy for Serious People

The Persons of the Play

Jack Worthing

Algernon Moncrieff

Rev. Canon Chasuble

Merriman, *butler*

Lane, *manservant*

Lady Bracknell

Hon. Gwendolen Fairfax

Cecily Cardew

Miss Prism, *governess*

The Scenes of the Play

Act 1
Algernon Moncrieff's flat in Half-Moon Street

Act 2
The garden at the Manor House, Woolton

Act 3
Drawing-room at the Manor House, Woolton

Time
The Present (i.e. 1895)

ACT 1

ACT 1, PART 1

In this part of the act you will:

- Be introduced to **social class** as a key theme in the play.
- Meet two friends called **Algernon** and **Jack**.
- Create your own **pun**.

1. very fashionable street in London

SCENE

Morning-room in ALGERNON's flat in Half-Moon Street.[1] The room is luxuriously and artistically furnished. The sound of a piano is heard in the next room. LANE is arranging afternoon tea on the table and, after the music has stopped, ALGERNON enters [from music-room].

ALGERNON

Did you hear what I was playing, Lane?

LANE

I didn't think it polite to listen, sir.

2. correctly

3. feeling
4. strength/speciality

ALGERNON

I'm sorry for that, for your sake. I don't play accurately[2]—anyone can play accurately—but I play with wonderful expression. As far as the piano is concerned, sentiment[3] is my forte[4]. I keep science for Life.

LANE

Yes, sir.

ALGERNON

And, speaking of the science of Life, have you got the cucumber sandwiches cut for Lady Bracknell?

LANE

Yes, sir. [*Hands them on a salver*[5]]

5. flat tray made of silver

ALGERNON

[*Inspects them, takes two, and sits down on the sofa*] Oh! . . . by the way, Lane, I see from your book that on Thursday night, when Lord Shoreham and Mr Worthing were dining with me, eight bottles of champagne are entered as having been consumed[6].

6. drank

LANE

Yes, sir; eight bottles and a pint.

ALGERNON

Why is it that at a bachelor's[7] establishment[8] the servants invariably[9] drink the champagne? I ask merely[10] for information.

7. man who has never been married
8. home
9. always
10. only/just

LANE

I attribute[11] it to the superior quality of the wine, sir. I have often observed that in married households the champagne is rarely of a first-rate brand.

11. put it down to

ALGERNON

Good heavens! Is marriage so demoralising[12] as that?

12. disappointing

LANE

I believe it *is* a very pleasant state, sir. I have had very little experience of it myself up to the present. I have only been married once. That was in consequence[13] of a misunderstanding between myself and a young person.

13. due to

ALGERNON

[*Languidly*[14]] I don't know that I am much interested in your family life, Lane.

14. with little energy or strength

LANE

No, sir; it is not a very interesting subject. I never think of it myself.

ALGERNON

Very natural, I am sure. That will do, Lane, thank you.

LANE
Thank you, sir.

[*LANE goes out*]

ALGERNON
Lane's views on marriage seem somewhat lax[15]. Really, if the lower orders don't set us a good example, what on earth is the use of them? They seem, as a class, to have absolutely no sense of moral responsibility.

15. careless

[*Enter LANE*]

LANE
Mr Ernest Worthing.

[*Enter JACK. LANE goes out*]

ALGERNON
How are you, my dear Ernest? What brings you up to town?

JACK
Oh, pleasure, pleasure! What else should bring one anywhere? Eating as usual, I see, Algy!

ALGERNON
[*Stiffly*] I believe it is customary[16] in good society to take some slight refreshment[17] at five o'clock. Where have you been since last Thursday?

16. usual/traditional
17. light snack or drink

JACK
[*Sitting down on the sofa*] In the country.

ALGERNON
What on earth do you do there?

JACK
[*Pulling off his gloves*] When one is in town one amuses oneself. When one is in the country one amuses other people. It is excessively[18] boring.

18. very

ALGERNON
And who are the people you amuse?

JACK

[*Airily*] Oh, neighbours, neighbours.

ALGERNON

Got nice neighbours in your part of Shropshire[19]?

19. Shropshire is a county in the West Midlands of England.

JACK

Perfectly horrid! Never speak to one of them.

ALGERNON

How immensely[20] you must amuse them! [*Goes over and takes sandwich*] By the way, Shropshire is your county, is it not?

20. very much

JACK

Eh? Shropshire? Yes, of course. Hallo! Why all these cups? Why cucumber sandwiches? Why such reckless[21] extravagance[22] in one so young? Who is coming to tea?

21. careless
22. overspending/wastefulness

ALGERNON

Oh! merely Aunt Augusta and Gwendolen.

JACK

How perfectly delightful!

ALGERNON

Yes, that is all very well; but I am afraid Aunt Augusta won't quite approve of your being here.

JACK

May I ask why?

ALGERNON

My dear fellow, the way you flirt with Gwendolen is perfectly disgraceful. It is almost as bad as the way Gwendolen flirts with you.

JACK

I am in love with Gwendolen. I have come up to town expressly[23] to propose to her.

23. only

ALGERNON

I thought you had come up for pleasure? . . . I call that business.

JACK

How utterly unromantic you are!

ALGERNON

I really don't see anything romantic in proposing. It is very romantic to be in love. But there is nothing romantic about a definite proposal. Why, one may be accepted. One usually is, I believe. Then the excitement is all over. The very essence of romance is uncertainty. If ever I get married, I'll certainly try to forget the fact.

JACK

I have no doubt about that, dear Algy. The Divorce Court was specially invented for people whose memories are so curiously constituted[24].

24. put together

25. forming an idea without evidence

ALGERNON

Oh! there is no use speculating[25] on that subject. Divorces are made in Heaven—[*JACK puts out his hand to take a sandwich. ALGERNON at once interferes*] Please don't touch the cucumber sandwiches. They are ordered specially for Aunt Augusta. [*Takes one and eats it*]

JACK

Well, you have been eating them all the time.

ALGERNON

That is quite a different matter. She is my aunt. [*Takes plate from below*] Have some bread and butter. The bread and butter is for Gwendolen. Gwendolen is devoted[26] to bread and butter.

26. loyal

JACK

[*Advancing to table and helping himself*] And very good bread and butter it is too.

ALGERNON

Well, my dear fellow, you need not eat as if you were going to eat it all. You behave as if you were married to her already. You are not married to her already, and I don't think you ever will be.

JACK

Why on earth do you say that?

ALGERNON

Well, in the first place, girls never marry the men they flirt with. Girls don't think it right.

JACK

Oh, that is nonsense!

ALGERNON

It isn't. It is a great truth. It accounts for the extraordinary number of bachelors that one sees all over the place. In the second place, I don't give my consent[27].

27. permission

JACK

Your consent!

ALGERNON

My dear fellow, Gwendolen is my first cousin. And before I allow you to marry her, you will have to clear up the whole question of Cecily. [*Rings bell*]

JACK

Cecily! What on earth do you mean? What do you mean, Algy, by Cecily! I don't know anyone of the name of Cecily.

[*Enter LANE*]

ALGERNON

Bring me that cigarette case Mr Worthing left in the smoking-room the last time he dined here.

LANE

Yes, sir.

[*LANE goes out*]

JACK

Do you mean to say you have had my cigarette case all this time? I wish to goodness you had let me know. I have been writing frantic letters to Scotland Yard[28] about it. I was very nearly offering a large reward.

28. headquarters of the London police

ALGERNON

Well, I wish you would offer one. I happen to be more than usually hard up[29].

29. short of money

JACK

There is no good offering a large reward now that the thing is found.

[*Enter LANE with the cigarette case on a salver. ALGERNON takes it at once. Lane goes out*]

ALGERNON

I think that is rather mean of you, Ernest, I must say. [*Opens case and examines it*] However, it makes no matter, for, now that I look at the inscription[30] inside, I find that the thing isn't yours after all.

30. words written on an object, often given as a gift

JACK

Of course it's mine. [*Moving to him*] You have seen me with it a hundred times, and you have no right whatsoever to read what is written inside. It is a very ungentlemanly thing to read a private cigarette case.

ALGERNON

Oh! it is absurd³¹ to have a hard and fast rule about what one should read and what one shouldn't. More than half of modern culture depends on what one shouldn't read.

31. silly/illogical

JACK

I am quite aware of the fact, and I don't propose to discuss modern culture. It isn't the sort of thing one should talk of in private. I simply want my cigarette case back.

ALGERNON

Yes; but this isn't your cigarette case. This cigarette case is a present from someone of the name of Cecily, and you said you didn't know anyone of that name.

JACK

Well, if you want to know, Cecily happens to be my aunt.

ALGERNON

Your aunt!

JACK

Yes. Charming old lady she is, too. Lives at Tunbridge Wells. Just give it back to me, Algy.

ALGERNON

[*Retreating to back of sofa*] But why does she call herself little Cecily if she is your aunt and lives at Tunbridge Wells? [*Reading*] 'From little Cecily with her fondest love.'

JACK

[*Moving to sofa and kneeling upon it*] My dear fellow, what on earth is there in that? Some aunts are tall, some aunts are not tall. That is a matter that surely an aunt may be allowed to decide for herself. You seem to think that every aunt should be exactly like your aunt! That is absurd! For Heaven's sake give me back my cigarette case. [*Follows ALGERNON round the room*]

ALGERNON

Yes. But why does your aunt call you her uncle? 'From little Cecily, with her fondest love to her dear Uncle Jack.' There is no objection, I admit, to an aunt being a small aunt, but why an aunt, no matter what her size may be, should call her own nephew her uncle, I can't quite make out. Besides, your name isn't Jack at all; it is Ernest.

JACK

 It isn't Ernest; it's Jack.

ALGERNON

 You have always told me it was Ernest. I have introduced you to every one as Ernest. You answer to the name of Ernest. You look as if your name was Ernest. You are the most earnest[32] looking person I ever saw in my life. It is perfectly absurd your saying that your name isn't Ernest. It's on your cards. Here is one of them. [*Taking it from case*] 'Mr Ernest Worthing, B. 4, The Albany.' I'll keep this as a proof that your name is Ernest if ever you attempt to deny it to me, or to Gwendolen, or to anyone else. [*Puts the card in his pocket*]

JACK

Well, my name is Ernest in town and Jack in the country, and the cigarette case was given to me in the country.

ALGERNON

Yes, but that does not account for the fact that your small Aunt Cecily, who lives at Tunbridge Wells, calls you her dear uncle. Come, old boy, you had much better have the thing out at once.

JACK

My dear Algy, you talk exactly as if you were a dentist. It is very vulgar[33] to talk like a dentist when one isn't a dentist. It produces a false impression[34].

ALGERNON

Well, that is exactly what dentists always do. Now, go on! Tell me the whole thing. I may mention that I have always suspected you of being a confirmed and secret Bunburyist; and I am quite sure of it now.

JACK

Bunburyist? What on earth do you mean by a Bunburyist?

32. sincere/serious

33. tasteless

34. idea; also, in dentistry, a copy of teeth made by pressing them into a soft substance

ALGERNON

I'll reveal to you the meaning of that incomparable[35] expression as soon as you are kind enough to inform me why you are Ernest in town and Jack in the country.

JACK

Well, produce my cigarette case first.

ALGERNON

Here it is. [*Hands cigarette case*] Now produce your explanation, and pray make it improbable[36]. [*Sits on sofa*]

35. without compare

36. unlikely to be true

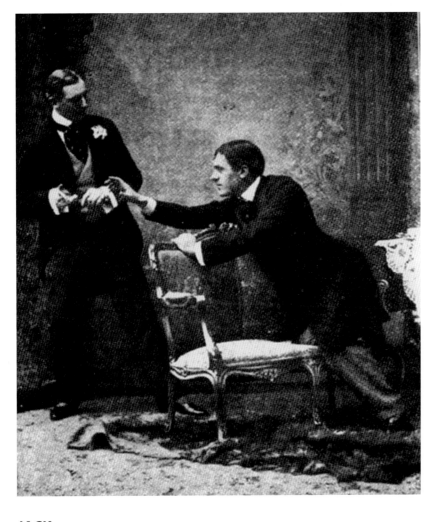

JACK

My dear fellow, there is nothing improbable about my explanation at all. In fact it's perfectly ordinary. Old Mr Thomas Cardew, who adopted me when I was a little boy, made me in his will guardian to his granddaughter, Miss Cecily Cardew. Cecily, who addresses me as her uncle from motives[37] of respect that you could not possibly appreciate, lives at my place in the country under the charge of her admirable governess[38], Miss Prism.

37. reasons

38. a woman employed to teach children in a private household

ALGERNON

Where is that place in the country, by the way?

JACK

That is nothing to you, dear boy. You are not going to be invited . . . I may tell you candidly[39] that the place is not in Shropshire.

39. truthfully

ALGERNON

I suspected that, my dear fellow! I have Bunburyed all over Shropshire on two separate occasions. Now, go on. Why are you Ernest in town and Jack in the country?

JACK

My dear Algy, I don't know whether you will be able to understand my real motives. You are hardly serious enough. When one is placed in the position of guardian, one has to adopt a very high moral tone on all subjects. It's one's duty to do so. And as a high moral tone can hardly be said to conduce[40] very much to either one's health or one's happiness, in order to get up to town I have always pretended to have a younger brother of the name of Ernest, who lives in the Albany, and gets into the most dreadful scrapes. That, my dear Algy, is the whole truth pure and simple.

40. bring/contribute

ALGERNON

The truth is rarely pure and never simple. Modern life would be very tedious[41] if it were either, and modern literature a complete impossibility!

41. boring

JACK

That wouldn't be at all a bad thing.

ALGERNON

Literary criticism[42] is not your forte, my dear fellow. Don't try it. You should leave that to people who haven't been at a University. They do it so well in the daily papers. What you really are is a Bunburyist. I was quite right in saying you were a Bunburyist. You are one of the most advanced Bunburyists I know.

42. the study of literature

JACK

What on earth do you mean?

ALGERNON

You have invented a very useful younger brother called Ernest, in order that you may be able to come up to town as often as you like. I have invented an invaluable[43] permanent invalid[44] called Bunbury, in order that I may be able to go down into the country whenever I choose. Bunbury is perfectly invaluable. If it wasn't for Bunbury's extraordinary bad health, for instance, I wouldn't be able to dine with you at Willis's tonight, for I have been really engaged to[45] Aunt Augusta for more than a week.

43. very useful
44. sick person

45. had plans with

JACK

I haven't asked you to dine with me anywhere tonight.

ALGERNON

I know. You are absurdly careless about sending out invitations. It is very foolish of you. Nothing annoys people so much as not receiving invitations.

JACK

You had much better dine with your Aunt Augusta.

ALGERNON

I haven't the smallest intention of doing anything of the kind. To begin with, I dined there on Monday, and once a week is quite enough to dine with one's own relations. In the second place, whenever I do dine there I am always treated as a member of the family, and sent down[46] with either no woman at all, or two. In the third place, I know perfectly well whom she will place me next to, tonight. She will place me next Mary Farquhar, who always flirts with her own husband across the dinner-table. That is not very pleasant. Indeed, it is not even decent . . . and that sort of thing is enormously on the increase. The amount of women in London who flirt with their own husbands is perfectly scandalous[47]. It looks so bad. It is simply washing one's clean linen in public. Besides, now that I know you to be a confirmed Bunburyist I naturally want to talk to you about Bunburying. I want to tell you the rules.

46. At formal Victorian dinners, guests gathered in the upstairs drawing room, where they were partnered in male/female pairs. The male guests then escorted their female partner downstairs to the dining room.

47. disgraceful/improper

JACK

I'm not a Bunburyist at all. If Gwendolen accepts me, I am going to kill my brother, indeed I think I'll kill him in any case. Cecily is a little too much interested in him. It is rather a bore. So I am going to get rid of Ernest. And I strongly advise you to do the same with Mr . . . with your invalid friend who has the absurd name.

48. convince

49. boring

50. judgementally
51. In Victorian England, French books and plays were thought to be immoral.
52. offering

53. negative

54. Wagner was a German composer, known for his emotional music.

ALGERNON

Nothing will induce[48] me to part with Bunbury, and if you ever get married, which seems to me extremely problematic, you will be very glad to know Bunbury. A man who marries without knowing Bunbury has a very tedious[49] time of it.

JACK

That is nonsense. If I marry a charming girl like Gwendolen, and she is the only girl I ever saw in my life that I would marry, I certainly won't want to know Bunbury.

ALGERNON

 Then your wife will. You don't seem to realise, that in married life three is company and two is none.

JACK

[*Sententiously*[50]] That, my dear young friend, is the theory that the corrupt French Drama[51] has been propounding[52] for the last fifty years.

ALGERNON

Yes; and that the happy English home has proved in half the time.

JACK

For heaven's sake, don't try to be cynical[53]. It's perfectly easy to be cynical.

ALGERNON

My dear fellow, it isn't easy to be anything nowadays. There's such a lot of beastly competition about. [*The sound of an electric bell is heard*] Ah! that must be Aunt Augusta. Only relatives, or creditors, ever ring in that Wagnerian[54] manner. Now, if I get her out of the way for ten minutes, so that you can have an opportunity for proposing to Gwendolen, may I dine with you tonight at Willis's?

JACK

I suppose so, if you want to.

ALGERNON

Yes, but you must be serious about it. I hate people who are not serious about meals. It is so shallow of them.

ACTION SUMMARY ACT 1, PART 1

- Algernon is in his fashionable London home with his servant Lane. He is getting ready for his Aunt Augusta to arrive.
- Algernon's friend Ernest arrives. He plans to propose to Algernon's cousin Gwendolen.
- Algernon has a cigarette case that belongs to his friend. The writing in the case helps Algernon to find out that his friend's real name is Jack.
- Algernon reveals that he has invented a sick friend called Bunbury. When he wants to get out of something, he pretends he has to visit Bunbury.
- Algernon calls Jack a Bunburyist (a person who has made up a fake character so they can live a double life).
- Jack tells Algernon that he is the legal guardian of a young woman named Cecily Cardew. He invented a younger brother, Ernest, so he could come to London and have fun without Cecily knowing.
- Jack says that he will kill Ernest off if Gwendolen agrees to marry him.
- Algernon says that he could never give up Bunburying.

A. REVIEWING

1. How do we know that Algernon is upper class?
2. What are your first impressions of Algernon?
3. Who does Algernon order the cucumber sandwiches for? What happens to the sandwiches?
4. Why does Jack pretend to have a younger brother called Ernest?
5. What is Bunburying?

B. EXPLORING

What's in a Name?

In Act 1 we are introduced to Jack, one of the play's main characters. However, at the beginning of the play the other characters know him as Ernest Worthing.

1. Use a dictionary to find the meaning of the words 'earnest' and 'worth'.
2. What would you expect a character with this name to be like? Are these things true of Jack so far?

Turn to **page 7** of your portfolio to record your answers.

C. ORAL LANGUAGE

The Importance of Being Witty

Group Activity

Oscar Wilde is famous for his wit and *The Importance of Being Earnest* is full of witty humour.

1. In groups, discuss why Lane's opening line is witty.

2. Can you find any other examples of witty dialogue in the first part of Act 1? Which did you find the funniest?

D. CREATING

1. Go Wilde With Puns

A pun is a play on words that sound the same but have different meanings. Oscar Wilde uses many puns in his writing. Puns provide comedy, but they can also add double meaning to what characters are saying.

The Importance of Being Earnest plays on the fact that the name Ernest sounds exactly the same as the word 'earnest', which means being sincere. For example, when Algernon discovers in Act 1 that Jack has been lying about his name, Algernon says:

> You look as if your name was Ernest. You are the most earnest looking person I ever saw in my life.

Of course, by lying about his name, Jack has not been sincere!

Turn to **page 9** of your portfolio to make a pun of your own.

2. Truth and Lies

Pair Activity

In Act 1 Algernon says, 'The truth is rarely pure and never simple.'

a. Turn to **page 10** of your portfolio. Using the grid provided, write ten statements about yourself. Make five of these statements lies and five of these statements truths.

b. Once you have written your statements, read them to your partner. They must guess which statements are true and which are false. You should then listen to your partner's statements and do the same.

Remember, make your truths exciting and deliver your lies convincingly!

In this part of the act you will:

- Meet **Lady Bracknell**, Algernon's Aunt.
- Meet **Gwendolen Fairfax**, Lady Bracknell's daughter.
- See that Gwendolen and Jack are in **love** with each other.
- Find out more about **marriage** in upper-class Victorian society.

[*Enter LANE*]

LANE

Lady Bracknell and Miss Fairfax.

[*ALGERNON goes forward to meet them. Enter LADY BRACKNELL and GWENDOLEN*]

LADY BRACKNELL

Good afternoon, dear Algernon, I hope you are behaving very well.

ALGERNON

I'm feeling very well, Aunt Augusta.

LADY BRACKNELL

That's not quite the same thing. In fact the two things rarely go together. [*Sees JACK and bows to him with icy coldness*]

ALGERNON

[*To GWENDOLEN*] Dear me, you are smart!

GWENDOLEN

I am always smart! Aren't I, Mr Worthing?

JACK

You're quite perfect, Miss Fairfax.

GWENDOLEN

Oh! I hope I am not that. It would leave no room for developments, and I intend to develop in many directions. [*GWENDOLEN and JACK sit down together in the corner*]

ACT 1, PART 2 ⟿

LADY BRACKNELL

I'm sorry if we are a little late, Algernon, but I was obliged to call on dear Lady Harbury. I hadn't been there since her poor husband's death. I never saw a woman so altered[1]; she looks quite twenty years younger. And now I'll have a cup of tea, and one of those nice cucumber sandwiches you promised me.

ALGERNON

Certainly, Aunt Augusta. [*Goes over to tea-table*]

LADY BRACKNELL

Won't you come and sit here, Gwendolen?

GWENDOLEN

Thanks, mamma, I'm quite comfortable where I am.

ALGERNON

[*Picking up empty plate in horror*] Good heavens! Lane! Why are there no cucumber sandwiches? I ordered them specially.

LANE

[*Gravely[2]*] There were no cucumbers in the market this morning, sir. I went down twice.

ALGERNON

No cucumbers!

LANE

No, sir. Not even for ready money[3].

ALGERNON

That will do, Lane, thank you.

LANE

Thank you, sir. [Goes out]

ALGERNON

I am greatly distressed, Aunt Augusta, about there being no cucumbers, not even for ready money.

1. changed

2. seriously

3. cash

18 THE IMPORTANCE OF BEING EARNEST

LADY BRACKNELL

It really makes no matter, Algernon. I had some crumpets with Lady Harbury, who seems to me to be living entirely for pleasure now.

ALGERNON

I hear her hair has turned quite gold from grief.

LADY BRACKNELL

It certainly has changed its colour. From what cause I, of course, cannot say. [*ALGERNON crosses and hands tea*] Thank you. I've quite a treat for you tonight, Algernon. I am going to send you down with Mary Farquhar. She is such a nice woman, and so attentive to her husband. It's delightful to watch them.

ALGERNON

I am afraid, Aunt Augusta, I shall have to give up the pleasure of dining with you tonight after all.

LADY BRACKNELL

[*Frowning*] I hope not, Algernon. It would put my table completely out. Your uncle would have to dine upstairs. Fortunately he is accustomed[4] to that.

4. used

ALGERNON

It is a great bore, and, I need hardly say, a terrible disappointment to me, but the fact is I have just had a telegram[5] to say that my poor friend Bunbury is very ill again. [*Exchanges glances with JACK*] They seem to think I should be with him.

LADY BRACKNELL

It is very strange. This Mr Bunbury seems to suffer from curiously[6] bad health.

ALGERNON

Yes; poor Bunbury is a dreadful invalid.

LADY BRACKNELL

Well, I must say, Algernon, that I think it is high time that Mr Bunbury made up his mind whether he was going to live or to die. This shilly-shallying[7] with the question is absurd. Nor do I in any way approve of the modern sympathy with invalids. I consider it morbid[8]. Illness of any kind is hardly a thing to be encouraged in others. Health is the primary duty of life. I am always telling that to your poor uncle, but he never seems to take much notice . . . as far as any improvement in his ailments[9] goes. I should be much obliged[10] if you would ask Mr Bunbury, from me, to be kind enough not to have a relapse[11] on Saturday, for I rely on you to arrange my music for me. It is my last reception, and one wants something that will encourage conversation, particularly at the end of the season[12] when everyone has practically said whatever they had to say, which, in most cases, was probably not much.

ALGERNON

I'll speak to Bunbury, Aunt Augusta, if he is still conscious, and I think I can promise you he'll be all right by Saturday. Of course the music is a great difficulty. You see, if one plays good music, people don't listen, and if one plays bad music people don't talk. But I'll run over the programme I've drawn out, if you will kindly come into the next room for a moment.

5. message sent by electrical wires

6. strangely

7. uncertainty/back and forth

8. an unhealthy interest in disease and death

9. minor illnesses

10. grateful
11. become ill gain

12. The social season was the part of the year when the Victorian upper class held balls and parties.

LADY BRACKNELL

Thank you, Algernon. It is very thoughtful of you. [*Rising, and following ALGERNON*] I'm sure the programme will be delightful, after a few expurgations.[13] French songs I cannot possibly allow. People always seem to think that they are improper, and either look shocked, which is vulgar, or laugh, which is worse. But German sounds a thoroughly respectable language, and indeed, I believe is so. Gwendolen, you will accompany me.

GWENDOLEN

Certainly, mamma.

[*LADY BRACKNELL and ALGERNON go into the music-room, Gwendolen remains behind*]

JACK

Charming day it has been, Miss Fairfax.

GWENDOLEN

Pray don't talk to me about the weather, Mr Worthing. Whenever people talk to me about the weather, I always feel quite certain that they mean something else. And that makes me so nervous.

JACK

I do mean something else.

GWENDOLEN

I thought so. In fact, I am never wrong.

JACK

And I would like to be allowed to take advantage of Lady Bracknell's temporary absence . . .

GWENDOLEN

I would certainly advise you to do so. Mamma has a way of coming back suddenly into a room that I have often had to speak to her about.

JACK

[*Nervously*] Miss Fairfax, ever since I met you I have admired you more than any girl . . . I have ever met since . . . I met you.

13. to remove rude or unsuitable material from something, such as a book

GWENDOLEN

Yes, I am quite aware of the fact. And I often wish that in public, at any rate, you had been more demonstrative[14]. For me you have always had an irresistible fascination[15]. Even before I met you I was far from indifferent to[16] you. [*JACK looks at her in amazement*] We live, as I hope you know, Mr Worthing, in an age of ideals. The fact is constantly mentioned in the more expensive monthly magazines, and has reached the provincial[17] pulpits, I am told; and my ideal has always been to love someone of the name of Ernest. There is something in that name that inspires absolute confidence. The moment Algernon first mentioned to me that he had a friend called Ernest, I knew I was destined to love you.

JACK

You really love me, Gwendolen?

GWENDOLEN

Passionately!

JACK

Darling! You don't know how happy you've made me.

GWENDOLEN

My own Ernest!

JACK

But you don't really mean to say that you couldn't love me if my name wasn't Ernest?

GWENDOLEN

But your name is Ernest.

JACK

Yes, I know it is. But supposing it was something else? Do you mean to say you couldn't love me then?

GWENDOLEN

[*Glibly*[18]] Ah! that is clearly a metaphysical[19] speculation, and like most metaphysical speculations has very little reference at all to the actual facts of real life, as we know them.

18. insincerely
19. abstract/not real

JACK

Personally, darling, to speak quite candidly[20], I don't much care about the name of Ernest . . . I don't think the name suits me at all.

20. honestly

GWENDOLEN

It suits you perfectly. It is a divine name. It has a music of its own. It produces vibrations.

JACK

Well, really, Gwendolen, I must say that I think there are lots of other much nicer names. I think Jack, for instance, a charming name.

GWENDOLEN

Jack? . . . No, there is very little music in the name Jack, if any at all, indeed. It does not thrill. It produces absolutely no vibrations . . . I have known several Jacks, and they all, without exception, were more than usually plain. Besides, Jack is a notorious domesticity[21] for John! And I pity any woman who is married to a man called John. She would probably never be allowed to know the entrancing pleasure of a single moment's solitude[22]. The only really safe name is Ernest.

21. common version

 22. peace and quiet

JACK

Gwendolen, I must get christened at once—I mean we must get married at once. There is no time to be lost.

GWENDOLEN

Married, Mr Worthing?

JACK

[*Astounded*] Well . . . surely. You know that I love you, and you led me to believe, Miss Fairfax, that you were not absolutely indifferent to me.

GWENDOLEN

I adore you. But you haven't proposed to me yet. Nothing has been said at all about marriage. The subject has not even been touched on.

JACK

Well . . . may I propose to you now?

GWENDOLEN

I think it would be an admirable opportunity. And to spare you any possible disappointment, Mr Worthing, I think it only fair to tell you quite frankly beforehand that I am fully determined to accept you.

JACK

Gwendolen!

GWENDOLEN

Yes, Mr Worthing, what have you got to say to me?

JACK

You know what I have got to say to you.

GWENDOLEN

Yes, but you don't say it.

JACK

Gwendolen, will you marry me? [*Goes on his knees*]

GWENDOLEN

Of course I will, darling. How long you have been about it! I am afraid you have had very little experience in how to propose.

JACK

 My own one, I have never loved anyone in the world but you.

GWENDOLEN

Yes, but men often propose for practice. I know my brother Gerald does. All my girl-friends tell me so. What wonderfully blue eyes you have, Ernest! They are quite, quite, blue. I hope you will always look at me just like that, especially when there are other people present.

[*Enter LADY BRACKNELL*]

LADY BRACKNELL

Mr Worthing! Rise, sir, from this semi-recumbent[23] posture. It is most indecorous[24].

23. almost lying down
24. in poor taste

GWENDOLEN

Mamma! [*He tries to rise; she restrains him*] I must beg you to retire. This is no place for you. Besides, Mr Worthing has not quite finished yet.

LADY BRACKNELL

Finished what, may I ask?

GWENDOLEN

I am engaged to Mr Worthing, mamma. [*They rise together*]

LADY BRACKNELL

Pardon me, you are not engaged to anyone. When you do become engaged to someone, I, or your father, should his health permit him, will inform you of the fact. An engagement should come on a young girl as a surprise, pleasant or unpleasant, as the case may be. It is hardly a matter that she could be allowed to arrange for herself . . . And now I have a few questions to put to you, Mr Worthing. While I am making these inquiries, you, Gwendolen, will wait for me below in the carriage.

GWENDOLEN

[*Reproachfully*25] Mamma!

25. critically

LADY BRACKNELL

In the carriage, Gwendolen! [*GWENDOLEN goes to the door. She and JACK blow kisses to each other behind LADY BRACKNELL's back. LADY BRACKNELL looks vaguely about as if she could not understand what the noise was. Finally turns round*] Gwendolen, the carriage!

GWENDOLEN

Yes, mamma. [*Goes out, looking back at JACK*]

LADY BRACKNELL

[*Sitting down*] You can take a seat, Mr Worthing. [*Looks in her pocket for note-book and pencil*]

JACK

Thank you, Lady Bracknell, I prefer standing.

LADY BRACKNELL

[*Pencil and note-book in hand*] I feel bound to tell you that you are not down on my list of eligible26 young men, although I have the same list as the dear Duchess of Bolton has. We work together, in fact. However, I am quite ready to enter your name, should your answers be what a really affectionate mother requires. Do you smoke?

26. suitable for marriage

JACK

Well, yes, I must admit I smoke.27

27. Smoking was a pastime for upper-class men in Victorian England. They bought special pipes and cases for their tobacco and even wore smoking jackets made from velvet or silk.

LADY BRACKNELL

I am glad to hear it. A man should always have an occupation28 of some kind. There are far too many idle men in London as it is. How old are you?

28. something to keep him busy

JACK

Twenty-nine.

LADY BRACKNELL

A very good age to be married at. I have always been of opinion that a man who desires to get married should know either everything or nothing. Which do you know?

JACK

[*After some hesitation*] I know nothing, Lady Bracknell.

LADY BRACKNELL

I am pleased to hear it. I do not approve of anything that tampers with natural ignorance. Ignorance is like a delicate exotic fruit; touch it and the bloom is gone. The whole theory of modern education is radically unsound. Fortunately in England, at any rate, education produces no effect whatsoever. If it did, it would prove a serious danger to the upper classes, and probably lead to acts of violence in Grosvenor Square. What is your income?

JACK

Between seven and eight thousand a year.

LADY BRACKNELL

[*Makes a note in her book*] In land, or in investments?

JACK

In investments, chiefly[29].

29. mainly

LADY BRACKNELL

That is satisfactory[30]. What between the duties[31] expected of one during one's lifetime, and the duties[32] exacted from one after one's death, land has ceased to be either a profit or a pleasure. It gives one position, and prevents one from keeping it up. That's all that can be said about land.

30. acceptable
31. responsibilities
32. taxes

JACK

I have a country house with some land, of course, attached to it, about fifteen hundred acres, I believe; but I don't depend on that for my real income. In fact, as far as I can make out, the poachers[33] are the only people who make anything out of it.

33. illegal hunters

LADY BRACKNELL

A country house! How many bedrooms? Well, that point can be cleared up afterwards. You have a town house, I hope? A girl with a simple, unspoiled nature, like Gwendolen, could hardly be expected to reside in the country.

JACK

Well, I own a house in Belgrave Square, but it is let by the year to Lady Bloxham. Of course, I can get it back whenever I like, at six months' notice.

LADY BRACKNELL

Lady Bloxham? I don't know her.

JACK

Oh, she goes about very little. She is a lady considerably advanced in years.

LADY BRACKNELL

Ah, nowadays that is no guarantee of respectability of character. What number in Belgrave Square?

JACK

149.

LADY BRACKNELL

[*Shaking her head*] The unfashionable side. I thought there was something. However, that could easily be altered.

JACK

Do you mean the fashion, or the side?

LADY BRACKNELL

[*Sternly*] Both, if necessary, I presume. What are your politics?

JACK

Well, I am afraid I really have none. I am a Liberal Unionist[34].

34. The Liberal Unionists were a conservative English political party.

LADY BRACKNELL

Oh, they count as Tories.[35] They dine with us. Or come in the evening, at any rate. Now to minor matters. Are your parents living?

35. an English political party traditionally associated with the upper classes

JACK

I have lost both my parents.

LADY BRACKNELL

To lose one parent, Mr Worthing, may be regarded as a misfortune; to lose both looks like carelessness. Who was your father? He was evidently[36] a man of some wealth. Was he born in what the Radical papers call the purple of commerce, or did he rise from the ranks of the aristocracy?

36. clearly

JACK

I am afraid I really don't know. The fact is, Lady Bracknell, I said I had lost my parents. It would be nearer the truth to say that my parents seem to have lost me . . . I don't actually know who I am by birth. I was . . . well, I was found.

LADY BRACKNELL

Found!

JACK

The late Mr Thomas Cardew, an old gentleman of a very charitable and kindly disposition, found me, and gave me the name of Worthing, because he happened to have a first-class ticket for Worthing in his pocket at the time. Worthing is a place in Sussex. It is a seaside resort.

LADY BRACKNELL

Where did the charitable gentleman who had a first-class ticket for this seaside resort find you?

JACK

[*Gravely*] In a hand-bag.

LADY BRACKNELL

A hand-bag?

JACK

[*Very seriously*] Yes, Lady Bracknell. I was in a hand-bag—a somewhat large, black leather hand-bag, with handles to it—an ordinary hand-bag in fact.

LADY BRACKNELL

In what locality did this Mr James, or Thomas, Cardew come across this ordinary hand-bag?

JACK

In the cloak-room at Victoria Station. It was given to him in mistake for his own.

LADY BRACKNELL

The cloak-room at Victoria Station?

JACK

Yes. The Brighton line.

LADY BRACKNELL

The line is immaterial[37]. Mr Worthing, I confess I feel somewhat bewildered[38] by what you have just told me. To be born, or at any rate bred, in a hand-bag, whether it had handles or not, seems to me to display a contempt[39] for the ordinary decencies of family life that reminds one of the worst excesses of the French Revolution[40].

37. not important
38. confused
39. disrespect
40. An uprising of the lower classes against the upper classes in France that took place in the late eighteenth century. The royal family were done away with and France became a republic.

And I presume you know what that unfortunate movement led to?
As for the particular locality[41] in which the hand-bag was found,
a cloak-room at a railway station might serve to conceal[42] a social
indiscretion[43]—has probably, indeed, been used for that purpose
before now—but it could hardly be regarded as an assured basis for
a recognised position in good society.

JACK

May I ask you then what you would advise me to do? I need hardly
say I would do anything in the world to ensure Gwendolen's
happiness.

LADY BRACKNELL

I would strongly advise you, Mr Worthing, to try and acquire[44]
some relations as soon as possible, and to make a definite effort to
produce at any rate one parent, of either sex, before the season[45] is
quite over.

JACK

Well, I don't see how I could possibly manage to do that. I can
produce the hand-bag at any moment. It is in my dressing-room at
home. I really think that should satisfy you, Lady Bracknell.

LADY BRACKNELL

Me, sir! What has it to do with me? You can hardly imagine that I and
Lord Bracknell would dream of allowing our only daughter—a girl
brought up with the utmost care—to marry into a cloak-room, and
form an alliance[46] with a parcel? Good morning, Mr Worthing!

[*LADY BRACKNELL sweeps out in majestic indignation[47]*]

41. place
42. hide
43. error
44. get
45. The social season was a good time for girls of marriageable age to meet suitable young men.
46. relationship
47. anger

ACTION SUMMARY
ACT 1, PART 2

- Algernon apologises to Lady Bracknell because there are no cucumber sandwiches. Lane lies that there were no cucumbers for sale at the market that morning.

- Algernon tells Lady Bracknell that he cannot have dinner with her because Bunbury is sick.

- Algernon takes Lady Bracknell out of the room so Jack and Gwendolen can be alone.

- Gwendolen tells Jack that she has always wanted to marry a man called Ernest.

- Gwendolen agrees to marry Jack, but only once she is satisfied that he has proposed in the correct way.

- Lady Bracknell returns and tells Gwendolen that she cannot be engaged without her permission.

- Lady Bracknell questions Jack about his wealth, politics and family to see if he is suitable for marriage.

- All is going well until Lady Bracknell finds out that Jack was abandoned in a train station as a baby. Jack's inability to prove his family history makes Lady Bracknell angry and she leaves.

A. REVIEWING

1. What are your first impressions of Lady Bracknell? Give examples to support your opinion.

2. Why does Gwendolen want to sit beside Jack?

3. What does Lane and Algernon's conversation about the cucumber sandwiches tell us about their relationship?

4. Why does Algernon take Lady Bracknell into the next room?

5. 'But you don't really mean to say that you couldn't love me if my name wasn't Ernest?' Why is Jack's question so important?

6. Do you think Gwendolen and Jack make a good couple? Why or why not?

B. EXPLORING

1. Who's Who?

Once you have read the first two parts of Act 1, turn to **page 11** of your portfolio. Using the diagram, see if you can link the characters by their relationships.

2. Researching Victorian Marriage

Group Activity

In this part of Act 2, we get an idea of the many rules that surrounded marriage in upper-class Victorian society.

a. Split the class into four groups. Each group should research one of the following aspects of marriage in upper-class Victorian society:

- The social season
- Courtship
- Engagement
- Weddings

b. In the order listed above, each group should give a presentation to the class.

C. CREATING

Banter

Banter is when people tease each other in a friendly way.

Turn to **page 12** of your portfolio and use the grid to give three examples of banter from the first two parts of Act 1.

1. Explain why each of your choices is a good example of banter. (Remember that banter is friendly.)

2. Suggest a modern replacement for each of your choices. To do this, think about how you banter with your friends.

ACT 1, PART 3

In this part of the act you will:

- Learn more about the theme of **secrets and lies**.
- Consider what Algernon is planning at the end of Act 1.

1. the music that plays as the bride enters a wedding, or as the bride and groom leave a wedding

JACK

Good morning! [*ALGERNON, from the other room, strikes up the Wedding March*[1]. *JACK looks perfectly furious, and goes to the door*] For goodness' sake don't play that ghastly tune, Algy! How idiotic you are!

[*The music stops and ALGERNON enters cheerily*]

ALGERNON

Didn't it go off all right, old boy? You don't mean to say Gwendolen refused you? I know it is a way she has. She is always refusing people. I think it is most ill-natured of her.

JACK

2. an object that gives physical support

3. a monster from Greek myth with snakes for hair

Oh, Gwendolen is as right as a trivet[2]. As far as she is concerned, we are engaged. Her mother is perfectly unbearable. Never met such a Gorgon[3] . . . I don't really know what a Gorgon is like, but I am quite sure that Lady Bracknell is one. In any case, she is a monster, without being a myth, which is rather unfair . . . I beg your pardon, Algy, I suppose I shouldn't talk about your own aunt in that way before you.

ALGERNON

My dear boy, I love hearing my relations abused. It is the only thing that makes me put up with them at all. Relations are simply a tedious pack of people, who haven't got the remotest knowledge of how to live, nor the smallest instinct about when to die.

JACK

Oh, that is nonsense!

ALGERNON

It isn't!

JACK

Well, I won't argue about the matter. You always want to argue about things.

ALGERNON

That is exactly what things were originally made for.

JACK

Upon my word, if I thought that, I'd shoot myself . . . [*A pause*] You don't think there is any chance of Gwendolen becoming like her mother in about a hundred and fifty years, do you, Algy?

ALGERNON

All women become like their mothers. That is their tragedy. No man does. That's his.

JACK

Is that clever?

ALGERNON

It is perfectly phrased! and quite as true as any observation in civilised life should be.

JACK

I am sick to death of cleverness. Everybody is clever nowadays. You can't go anywhere without meeting clever people. The thing has become an absolute public nuisance. I wish to goodness we had a few fools left.

ALGERNON

We have.

JACK

I should extremely like to meet them. What do they talk about?

ALGERNON

The fools? Oh! about the clever people, of course.

JACK

What fools!

ALGERNON

By the way, did you tell Gwendolen the truth about your being Ernest in town, and Jack in the country?

JACK

4. superior/rude

5. sophisticated

[*In a very patronising*[4] *manner*] My dear fellow, the truth isn't quite the sort of thing one tells to a nice, sweet, refined[5] girl. What extraordinary ideas you have about the way to behave to a woman!

ALGERNON

6. pay loving attention

The only way to behave to a woman is to make love[6] to her, if she is pretty, and to someone else, if she is plain.

JACK

Oh, that is nonsense.

ALGERNON

7. extravagant, immoral

What about your brother? What about the profligate[7] Ernest?

JACK

8. stroke

Oh, before the end of the week I shall have got rid of him. I'll say he died in Paris of apoplexy[8]. Lots of people die of apoplexy, quite suddenly, don't they?

ALGERNON

9. a condition passed from parent to child

Yes, but it's hereditary[9], my dear fellow. It's a sort of thing that runs in families. You had much better say a severe chill.

JACK

You are sure a severe chill isn't hereditary, or anything of that kind?

ALGERNON

Of course it isn't!

JACK

Very well, then. My poor brother Ernest to carried off suddenly, in Paris, by a severe chill. That gets rid of him.

ALGERNON

But I thought you said that . . . Miss Cardew was a little too much interested in your poor brother Ernest? Won't she feel his loss a good deal?

JACK

Oh, that is all right. Cecily is not a silly romantic girl, I am glad to say. She has got a capital[10] appetite, goes on long walks, and pays no attention at all to her lessons.

10. very good

ALGERNON

I would rather like to see Cecily.

JACK

I will take very good care you never do. She is excessively[11] pretty, and she is only just eighteen.

11. very/unusually

ALGERNON

Have you told Gwendolen yet that you have an excessively pretty ward[12] who is only just eighteen?

12. someone placed under the protection of a legal guardian

JACK

Oh! one doesn't blurt these things out to people. Cecily and Gwendolen are perfectly certain to be extremely great friends. I'll bet you anything you like that half an hour after they have met, they will be calling each other sister.

ALGERNON

Women only do that when they have called each other a lot of other things first. Now, my dear boy, if we want to get a good table at Willis's, we really must go and dress. Do you know it is nearly seven?

JACK

[*Irritably*] Oh! it always is nearly seven.

ALGERNON

Well, I'm hungry.

JACK

I never knew you when you weren't . . .

ALGERNON

What shall we do after dinner? Go to a theatre?

JACK

Oh no! I loathe[13] listening.

13. hate

ALGERNON

Well, let us go to the Club[14]?

14. A private gentlemen's club. These members-only clubs were very popular among upper-class men in Victorian London.

JACK

Oh, no! I hate talking.

ALGERNON

Well, we might trot round to the Empire[15] at ten?

15. a famous London music-hall

JACK

Oh, no! I can't bear looking at things. It is so silly.

ALGERNON

Well, what shall we do?

JACK

Nothing!

ALGERNON

It is awfully hard work doing nothing. However, I don't mind hard work where there is no definite object of any kind.

[*Enter LANE*]

LANE

Miss Fairfax.

[*Enter GWENDOLEN. LANE goes out*]

ALGERNON

Gwendolen, upon my word!

GWENDOLEN

Algy, kindly turn your back. I have something very particular to say to Mr Worthing.

ALGERNON

Really, Gwendolen, I don't think I can allow this at all.

GWENDOLEN

Algy, you always adopt a strictly immoral attitude towards life. You are not quite old enough to do that. [*ALGERNON retires to the fireplace*]

JACK

My own darling!

GWENDOLEN

Ernest, we may never be married. From the expression on mamma's face I fear we never shall. Few parents nowadays pay any regard to what their children say to them. The old-fashioned respect for the young is fast dying out. Whatever influence I ever had over mamma, I lost at the age of three. But although she may prevent us from becoming man and wife, and I may marry someone else, and marry often, nothing that she can possibly do can alter my eternal[16] devotion[17] to you.

16. everlasting

17. loyalty

JACK

Dear Gwendolen!

GWENDOLEN

The story of your romantic origin, as related to me by mamma, with unpleasing comments, has naturally stirred the deeper fibres of my nature. Your Christian name has an irresistible fascination. The simplicity of your character makes you exquisitely[18] incomprehensible[19] to me. Your town address at the Albany I have. What is your address in the country?

18. charmingly

19. unable to be understood

JACK

The Manor House, Woolton, Hertfordshire.

[*ALGERNON, who has been carefully listening, smiles to himself, and writes the address on his shirt-cuff. Then picks up the Railway Guide*]

GWENDOLEN

There is a good postal service, I suppose? It may be necessary to do something desperate. That of course will require serious consideration. I will communicate with you daily.

JACK

My own one!

GWENDOLEN

How long do you remain in town?

JACK

Till Monday.

GWENDOLEN

Good! Algy, you may turn round now.

ALGERNON

Thanks, I've turned round already.

GWENDOLEN

You may also ring the bell.

[*Algernon rings bell*]

JACK

You will let me see you to your carriage, my own darling?

GWENDOLEN

Certainly.

JACK

[*To LANE, who now enters*] I will see Miss Fairfax out.

LANE

Yes, sir. [*JACK and GWENDOLEN go off*]

[*Lane presents several letters on a salver to ALGERNON. It is to be surmised[18] that they are bills, as ALGERNON, after looking at the envelopes, tears them up*]

20. thought

ALGERNON

A glass of sherry, Lane.

LANE

Yes, sir.

ALGERNON

Tomorrow, Lane, I'm going Bunburying.

LANE

Yes, sir.

ALGERNON

I shall probably not be back till Monday. You can put up my dress clothes, my smoking jacket, and all the Bunbury suits . . .

LANE

Yes, sir. [*Handing sherry*]

ALGERNON

I hope tomorrow will be a fine day, Lane.

LANE

It never is, sir.

ALGERNON

Lane, you're a perfect pessimist[21].

21. someone who expects the worst outcome

LANE

I do my best to give satisfaction, sir.

[*Enter JACK. LANE goes off*]

JACK

There's a sensible, intellectual girl! the only girl I ever cared for in my life. [*ALGERNON is laughing immoderately*[22]] What on earth are you so amused at?

22. uncontrollably

ALGERNON

Oh, I'm a little anxious about poor Bunbury, that is all.

JACK

If you don't take care, your friend Bunbury will get you into a serious scrape some day.

ALGERNON

I love scrapes. They are the only things that are never serious.

JACK

Oh, that's nonsense, Algy. You never talk anything but nonsense.

ALGERNON

Nobody ever does.

23. angrily

[*JACK looks indignantly*[23] *at him, and leaves the room. ALGERNON lights a cigarette, reads his shirt-cuff, and smiles*]

ACT ENDS

ACTION SUMMARY
ACT 1, PART 3

- Algernon plays the wedding march on the piano to make fun of Jack's marriage proposal.
- Jack and Algernon talk about love and women.
- Algernon tells Jack that he would like to meet Cecily. Jack says that he will never allow it.
- Gwendolen returns and swears her devotion to Jack.
- Algernon hears Jack giving Gwendolen his address in the countryside and makes a note of it on his shirt sleeve.
- Algernon tells Lane that he is going Bunburying the next day.
- The scene ends with Algernon smiling at Jack's address on his sleeve.

A. REVIEWING

1. What does this part of Act 1 tell us about Jack and Algernon's friendship?
2. Based on what Jack says about her, what kind of person do you think Cecily is?
3. Why does Gwendolen love Jack?

B. EXPLORING

What is Algernon Thinking?

In the following stage direction, Algernon overhears Jack's country address and writes it on his sleeve:

ALGERNON, who has been carefully listening, smiles to himself, and writes the address on his shirt-cuff. Then picks up the Railway Guide.

Turn to **page 13** of your portfolio and write what Algernon might be thinking into the thought bubble.

C. CREATING

Making a Gorgon

Talking about Lady Bracknell, Jack says that he 'Never met such a Gorgon'.

Turn to **page 14** of your portfolio and use the picture of the gorgon to write six reasons why the audience might like Lady Bracknell and six reasons why they might dislike her.

D. REFLECTING

1. Character File

Turn to the Character File section of your portfolio and record your impressions of **Algernon**, **Jack**, **Gwendolen** and **Lady Bracknell** based on Act 1.

2. Mapping the Plot

Pair Activity

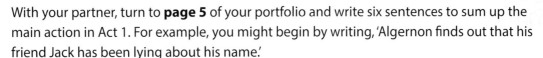

With your partner, turn to **page 5** of your portfolio and write six sentences to sum up the main action in Act 1. For example, you might begin by writing, 'Algernon finds out that his friend Jack has been lying about his name.'

3. Act 1 Word Search

Go to **page 26** of your portfolio to complete the Act 1 word search.

OVERVIEW OF ACT 1

Introducing Algernon Moncrieff

- When the play opens, Algernon Moncrieff is playing the piano in his fashionable London home. He doesn't play the piano very well, but he doesn't seem to care:

> *I don't play accurately—anyone can play accurately—but I play with wonderful expression.*

This celebration of **style over substance** is true of Algernon's character throughout the play. Indeed, this is one of the main criticisms that Oscar Wilde makes of the upper (wealthy) classes in the play: they champion **appearance and triviality** over what is truly important.

- Algernon's conversation with his servant Lane at the start of Act 1 introduces one of the play's main themes: **social class**. We see Algernon's disrespect of Lane's service when he eats the cucumber sandwiches that are meant for Lady Bracknell, then scolds Lane in front of the guests because there are none left. Lane plays along with this performance, showing that he knows his social place:

> *There were no cucumbers in the market this morning, sir. I went down twice.*

- During a **soliloquy** when Lane leaves the room in Act 1, Algernon accuses the lower classes of having 'absolutely no sense of moral responsibility'. His words are **ironic** because Algernon, an upper-class gentleman, seems to have very little sense of morality himself.

Jack Worthing comes clean

- Algernon is visited by his friend Jack Worthing. Jack is in love with Algernon's cousin Gwendolen Fairfax. He has come to London from the country to propose marriage to her.

- Although they are friends, Algernon has always known Jack by the name Ernest.

- Algernon has found a cigarette case belonging to Jack that has 'From little Cecily, with her fondest love to her dear Uncle Jack' written on it. When he asks Jack who Cecily is, Jack lies and says that she is his aunt.

- Jack reveals that he has been calling himself by the name Ernest when he comes to London so that he can have some fun. When he is in the countryside, he pretends that Ernest is his younger brother 'who gets into the most terrible scrapes'.

- The conversation about Jack's name introduces another of the play's main themes: **identity**. Algernon finds it hard to see past the name Ernest, which he believes perfectly sums up his friend:

> *You look as if your name was Ernest. You are the most earnest looking person I ever saw in my life. It is perfectly absurd your saying that your name isn't Ernest.*

The irrational idea that **the name makes the man** is continued throughout the play.

- Oscar Wilde makes a **pun** using the name Ernest and the word 'earnest', which means being sincere. This provides **comedy**, but it also adds **double meaning** to what the characters are saying when they talk about being earnest/Ernest.

- Jack tells Algernon about his past. When he was a child, he was adopted by a wealthy man called Thomas Cardew. When Thomas Cardew died, Jack was left his estate and became legal guardian of Cardew's granddaughter Cecily.

The art of Bunburying

- Algernon tells Jack that he has invented a fictional friend, a sick man called Bunbury. Algernon pretends to visit Bunbury when he wants to get out of something (such as having dinner with his aunt, Lady Bracknell).

> *Nothing will induce me to part with Bunbury…*

- Algernon calls leading a double life or keeping secrets **Bunburying**. He accuses Jack of being a **Bunburyist** because of his false identity as Ernest:

> … now that I know you to be a confirmed Bunburyist I naturally want to talk to you about Bunburying. I want to tell you the rules.

- When Lady Bracknell arrives, Algernon shows Bunburying in action when he tells her that he will be unable to have dinner with her that night because he has to visit his sick friend:

> I am afraid, Aunt Augusta, I shall have to give up the pleasure of dining with you tonight after all … but the fact is I have just had a telegram to say that my poor friend Bunbury is very ill again.

Jack and Gwendolen

- Algernon takes Lady Bracknell out of the room, leaving Jack and Gwendolen alone. Gwendolen agrees to marry Jack, but only once she is satisfied that he has proposed in the correct way. It is clear that Gwendolen considers society's rules about what is **proper** to be very important.

- Gwendolen also believes that Jack is called Ernest. She says that she has always wanted to marry a man named Ernest and explains that the name is the main reason for her **love**:

> …my ideal has always been to love some one of the name of Ernest. There is something in that name that inspires absolute confidence. The moment Algernon first mentioned to me that he had a friend called Ernest, I knew I was destined to love you.

- When Lady Bracknell returns to the room she tells Gwendolen that she cannot be engaged without her permission. In fact, she would rather choose Gwendolen's husband herself:

> Pardon me, you are not engaged to anyone. When you do become engaged to someone, I, or your father, should his health permit him, will inform you of the fact.

- Lady Bracknell is a **matriarch** (a strong female head of the family). She makes it very clear that all decisions, especially those about marriage, must be approved by her.

Lady Bracknell interrogates Jack

- **Marriage** was hugely important to the upper classes in Victorian England. A match with the right person guaranteed that a family's wealth and reputation would be maintained (and ideally improved).

- Lady Bracknell interviews Jack to see if he would make a suitable husband for her daughter. The interview reveals Lady Bracknell's **materialistic** side as she is delighted to hear of Jack's wealth.

- Everything is going well until Jack tells Lady Bracknell that he was found in a handbag in the cloakroom of a train station by Thomas Cardew. Worthing, Jack's surname, was the place Mr Cardew was travelling to. This is unforgivable to Lady Bracknell, as it means that Jack's parents are unknown and that he has no position in **society**:

> You can hardly imagine that I and Lord Bracknell would dream of allowing our only daughter—a girl brought up with the utmost care—to marry into a cloak-room, and form an alliance with a parcel? Good morning, Mr Worthing!

- Gwendolen shows that she loves Jack by returning to get his country address. She tells Jack that no matter what Lady Bracknell says, 'nothing that she can possibly do can alter my eternal devotion to you'.

The stage is set for Act 2

- Algernon overhears Jack's country address and tells Lane that he will be going Bunburying the next day.

- Algernon tells Jack, 'I love scrapes. They are the only things that are never serious.' This shows Algernon's flighty nature – it is clear that he thinks of life as a **game**. It also sets the stage for Act 2, which promises to include all manner of scrapes.

ACT 1 PROJECTS

Now that you have finished Act 1, you should reflect on what you have learned by doing *one* of the projects from options A and B below.

These projects will help you to prepare for the two Classroom Based Assessments (CBAs) you will complete as part of your Junior Cycle course.

Your first CBA will be an Oral Communication Task at the end of Second Year. Your second CBA will be a Collection of Texts Task in the middle of Third Year, which will involve selecting some of your written pieces.

A. Written Task

1. Choose one tone, one format and one character from the silver salver. Together, these things make up what you will write. For example, an amusing short story about Lane **or** an objective review of Jack's character.

Tone	Format	Character
Amusing	Letter	Algernon
Judgemental	Report	Jack
Sympathetic	Review	Gwendolen
Angry	Blog post	Lady Bracknell
Gloomy	Essay	Lane
Objective	Short story	

2. Go to **page 15** of your portfolio to give your writing task a title, plan it and write it. When you have finished, complete the student reflection note on **page 20** of your portfolio.

B. Oral Communication Task

Give a three-minute presentation to your class (two minutes to present and one minute for questions) on one of the following topics:

- My favourite character in Act 1
- The most important theme in Act 1

Go to **page 21** of your portfolio to plan your presentation. When you are finished, complete the student reflection note on **page 25** of your portfolio.

ACT 2

ACT 2, PART 1

In this part of the act you will:

- Meet a new main character, **Cecily Cardew**.
- Learn more about the theme of **social class** through the characters of **Merriman** (Cecily's butler), **Dr Chasuble** (the local canon) and **Miss Prism** (Cecily's governess).
- Develop your understanding of **symbols** and **dramatic irony**.

SCENE

Garden at the Manor House. A flight of grey stone steps leads up to the house. The garden, an old-fashioned one, full of roses. Time of year, July. Basket chairs, and a table covered with books, are set under a large yew-tree. MISS PRISM discovered seated at the table. CECILY is at the back, watering flowers.

MISS PRISM

[*Calling*] Cecily, Cecily! Surely such a utilitarian[1] occupation as the watering of flowers is rather Moulton's duty than yours? Especially at a moment when intellectual pleasures await you. Your German grammar is on the table. Pray open it at page fifteen. We will repeat yesterday's lesson.

CECILY

[*Coming over very slowly*] But I don't like German. It isn't at all a becoming[2] language. I know perfectly well that I look quite plain after my German lesson.

1. practical

2. attractive/flattering

MISS PRISM

Child, you know how anxious your guardian is that you should improve yourself in every way. He laid particular stress on your German, as he was leaving for town yesterday. Indeed, he always lays stress on your German when he is leaving for town.

CECILY

Dear Uncle Jack is so very serious! Sometimes he is so serious that I think he cannot be quite well.

MISS PRISM

[*Drawing herself up*] Your guardian enjoys the best of health, and his gravity of demeanour[3] is especially to be commended[4] in one so comparatively young as he is. I know no one who has a higher sense of duty and responsibility.

3. behaviour
4. praised

5. meaningless fun
6. unimportant things
7. worry

8. unable to be repaired
9. unable to make decisions

10. A Biblical reference to Galatians 6:7, meaning that how a person behaves will control what happens to them.

11. records

12. a London library

13. disrespectfully

CECILY

I suppose that is why he often looks a little bored when we three are together.

MISS PRISM

Cecily! I am surprised at you. Mr Worthing has many troubles in his life. Idle merriment[5] and triviality[6] would be out of place in his conversation. You must remember his constant anxiety[7] about that unfortunate young man his brother.

CECILY

I wish Uncle Jack would allow that unfortunate young man, his brother, to come down here sometimes. We might have a good influence over him, Miss Prism. I am sure you certainly would. You know German, and geology, and things of that kind influence a man very much. [*Cecily begins to write in her diary*]

MISS PRISM

[*Shaking her head*] I do not think that even I could produce any effect on a character that according to his own brother's admission is irretrievably[8] weak and vacillating[9]. Indeed I am not sure that I would desire to reclaim him. I am not in favour of this modern mania for turning bad people into good people at a moment's notice. As a man sows so let him reap[10]. You must put away your diary, Cecily. I really don't see why you should keep a diary at all.

CECILY

I keep a diary in order to enter the wonderful secrets of my life. If I didn't write them down, I should probably forget all about them.

MISS PRISM

Memory, my dear Cecily, is the diary that we all carry about with us.

CECILY

Yes, but it usually chronicles[11] the things that have never happened, and couldn't possibly have happened. I believe that Memory is responsible for nearly all the three-volume novels that Mudie[12] sends us.

MISS PRISM

Do not speak slightingly[13] of the three-volume novel, Cecily. I wrote one myself in earlier days.

CECILY

Did you really, Miss Prism? How wonderfully clever you are! I hope it did not end happily? I don't like novels that end happily. They depress me so much.

MISS PRISM

The good ended happily, and the bad unhappily. That is what Fiction means.

CECILY

I suppose so. But it seems very unfair. And was your novel ever published?

MISS PRISM

Alas! no. The manuscript[14] unfortunately was abandoned. [*CECILY starts*] I use the word in the sense of lost or mislaid. To your work, child, these speculations are profitless.

CECILY

[*Smiling*] But I see dear Dr Chasuble coming up through the garden.

14. not yet published book

MISS PRISM

[*Rising and advancing*] Dr Chasuble! This is indeed a pleasure.

[*Enter CANON CHASUBLE*[15]]

15. Dr Chasuble is a not a medical doctor. He is a canon. In the Church of England, this means he is a vicar with special responsibilities for marriages, deaths and baptisms. A chasuble is a garment worn by the clergy.

CHASUBLE

And how are we this morning? Miss Prism, you are, I trust, well?

CECILY

Miss Prism has just been complaining of a slight headache. I think it would do her so much good to have a short stroll with you in the Park, Dr Chasuble.

MISS PRISM

Cecily, I have not mentioned anything about a headache.

CECILY

No, dear Miss Prism, I know that, but I felt instinctively that you had a headache. Indeed I was thinking about that, and not about my German lesson, when the Rector came in.

CHASUBLE

I hope, Cecily, you are not inattentive[16].

16. failing to pay attention

CECILY

Oh, I am afraid I am.

CHASUBLE

That is strange. Were I fortunate enough to be Miss Prism's pupil, I would hang upon her lips. [*MISS PRISM glares*] I spoke metaphorically.—My metaphor was drawn from bees. Ahem! Mr Worthing, I suppose, has not returned from town yet?

MISS PRISM

We do not expect him till Monday afternoon.

CHASUBLE

Ah yes, he usually likes to spend his Sunday in London. He is not one of those whose sole aim is enjoyment, as, by all accounts, that unfortunate young man his brother seems to be. But I must not disturb Egeria[17] and her pupil any longer.

17. Egeria was a fourth-century woman who was religious and dedicated.

MISS PRISM

Egeria? My name is Laetitia, Doctor.

CHASUBLE

[*Bowing*] A classical allusion[18] merely, drawn from the Pagan authors.
I shall see you both no doubt at Evensong[19]?

MISS PRISM

I think, dear Doctor, I will have a stroll with you. I find I have a
headache after all, and a walk might do it good.

CHASUBLE

With pleasure, Miss Prism, with pleasure. We might go as far as the
schools and back.

MISS PRISM

That would be delightful. Cecily, you will read your Political
Economy in my absence. The chapter on the Fall of the Rupee[20]
you may omit[21]. It is somewhat too sensational. Even these metallic
problems have their melodramatic[22] side.

[*Goes down the garden with DR CHASUBLE*]

CECILY

[*Picks up books and throws them back on table*] Horrid Political
Economy! Horrid Geography! Horrid, horrid German!

[*Enter MERRIMAN with a card on a salver*]

MERRIMAN

Mr Ernest Worthing has just driven over from the station. He has
brought his luggage with him.

CECILY

[*Takes the card and reads it*] 'Mr Ernest Worthing, B. 4, The Albany, W.'
Uncle Jack's brother! Did you tell him Mr Worthing was in town?

MERRIMAN

Yes, Miss. He seemed very much disappointed. I mentioned that you
and Miss Prism were in the garden. He said he was anxious to speak
to you privately for a moment.

18. a reference to a Greek or Roman myth

19. evening prayer service

20. At the time the play was written, the Indian currency, the rupee, had been falling in value for twenty years.
21. leave out
22. exaggerated/overdramatic

CECILY

Ask Mr Ernest Worthing to come here. I suppose you had better talk to the housekeeper about a room for him.

MERRIMAN

Yes, Miss.

[*MERRIMAN goes off*]

CECILY

I have never met any really wicked person before. I feel rather frightened. I am so afraid he will look just like everyone else.

[*Enter ALGERNON, very gay[23] and debonair[24]*]

He does!

ALGERNON

[*Raising his hat*] You are my little cousin Cecily, I'm sure.

CECILY

You are under some strange mistake. I am not little. In fact, I believe I am more than usually tall for my age. [*ALGERNON is rather taken aback*] But I am your cousin Cecily. You, I see from your card, are Uncle Jack's brother, my cousin Ernest, my wicked cousin Ernest.

23. happy
24. elegant

ALGERNON

Oh! I am not really wicked at all, cousin Cecily. You mustn't think that I am wicked.

CECILY

If you are not, then you have certainly been deceiving us all in a very inexcusable[25] manner. I hope you have not been leading a double life, pretending to be wicked and being really good all the time. That would be hypocrisy[26].

25. unforgivable

26. doing things that you tell other people not to do

ALGERNON

[*Looks at her in amazement*] Oh! Of course I have been rather reckless.

CECILY

I am glad to hear it.

ALGERNON

In fact, now you mention the subject, I have been very bad in my own small way.

CECILY

I don't think you should be so proud of that, though I am sure it must have been very pleasant.

ALGERNON

It is much pleasanter being here with you.

CECILY

I can't understand how you are here at all. Uncle Jack won't be back till Monday afternoon.

ALGERNON

That is a great disappointment. I am obliged to go up by the first train on Monday morning. I have a business appointment that I am anxious . . . to miss!

CECILY

Couldn't you miss it anywhere but in London?

ALGERNON

No: the appointment is in London.

27. moving to another country

CECILY

Well, I know, of course, how important it is not to keep a business engagement, if one wants to retain any sense of the beauty of life, but still I think you had better wait till Uncle Jack arrives. I know he wants to speak to you about your emigrating[27].

ALGERNON

About my what?

CECILY

Your emigrating. He has gone up to buy your outfit.

ALGERNON

I certainly wouldn't let Jack buy my outfit. He has no taste in neckties at all.

CECILY

I don't think you will require neckties. Uncle Jack is sending you to Australia.

ALGERNON

Australia! I'd sooner die.

CECILY

Well, he said at dinner on Wednesday night, that you would have to choose between this world, the next world, and Australia.

ALGERNON

Oh, well! The accounts I have received of Australia and the next world, are not particularly encouraging. This world is good enough for me, cousin Cecily.

CECILY

Yes, but are you good enough for it?

ALGERNON

I'm afraid I'm not that. That is why I want you to reform[28] me. You might make that your mission, if you don't mind, cousin Cecily.

28. improve

CECILY

I'm afraid I've no time, this afternoon.

ALGERNON

Well, would you mind my reforming myself this afternoon?

CECILY

It is rather Quixotic[29] of you. But I think you should try.

29. idealistic/unrealistic

ALGERNON

I will. I feel better already.

CECILY

You are looking a little worse.

ALGERNON

That is because I am hungry.

CECILY

How thoughtless of me. I should have remembered that when one is going to lead an entirely new life, one requires regular and wholesome meals. Won't you come in?

30. Algernon is what the Victorians called a dandy. This means he puts a lot of importance on clothes and style. Victorian dandies often wore a flower in their buttonhole.

ALGERNON

Thank you. Might I have a buttonhole[30] first? I never have any appetite unless I have a buttonhole first.

31. yellow rose

CECILY

A Maréchal Niel[31]? [*Picks up scissors*]

ALGERNON

No, I'd sooner have a pink rose.

CECILY

Why? [*Cuts a flower*]

ALGERNON

Because you are like a pink rose, cousin Cecily.

CECILY

I don't think it can be right for you to talk to me like that. Miss Prism never says such things to me.

ALGERNON

Then Miss Prism is a short-sighted old lady. [*CECILY puts the rose in his buttonhole*] You are the prettiest girl I ever saw.

CECILY

Miss Prism says that all good looks are a snare.

ALGERNON

They are a snare that every sensible man would like to be caught in.

CECILY

Oh! I don't think I would care to catch a sensible man. I shouldn't know what to talk to him about.

[*They pass into the house. MISS PRISM and DR CHASUBLE return*]

MISS PRISM

You are too much alone, dear Dr Chasuble. You should get married. A misanthrope[32] I can understand—a womanthrope, never!

CHASUBLE

[*With a scholar's shudder*] Believe me, I do not deserve so neologistic[33] a phrase. The precept[34] as well as the practice of the Primitive Church was distinctly against matrimony[35].

MISS PRISM

[*Sententiously*[36]] That is obviously the reason why the Primitive Church has not lasted up to the present day. And you do not seem to realise, dear Doctor, that by persistently[37] remaining single, a man converts himself into a permanent public temptation. Men should be more careful; this very celibacy[38] leads weaker vessels astray.

CHASUBLE

But is a man not equally attractive when married?

MISS PRISM

No married man is ever attractive except to his wife.

CHASUBLE

And often, I've been told, not even to her.

MISS PRISM

That depends on the intellectual sympathies of the woman. Maturity can always be depended on. Ripeness can be trusted. Young women are green[39]. [*DR CHASUBLE starts*] I spoke horticulturally[40]. My metaphor was drawn from fruits. But where is Cecily?

CHASUBLE

Perhaps she followed us to the schools.

32. a person who dislikes other people and avoids company

33. a made-up, new word
34. rule
35. marriage

36. self-righteously

37. endlessly

38. not marrying

39. immature

40. in gardening terms

ACTION SUMMARY ACT 2, PART 1

- Cecily Cardew is in the garden of her Manor House having a lesson with her governess (tutor), Miss Prism.

- Cecily does not seem to be fully concentrating on her lesson as she is worrying about her guardian, Jack.

- When Miss Prism notices Cecily writing in her diary she asks why she bothers keeping one. Cecily tells her that it is a way to remember her greatest secrets.

- Miss Prism reveals that she wrote a three-volume novel when she was younger but the manuscript was lost.

- Dr Chasuble, the local canon, arrives. He and Miss Prism flirt with one another, before leaving together for a walk down the garden.

- Cecily's butler, Merriman, enters to inform her that Jack's brother Ernest has arrived. This is in fact Algernon, Bunburying as Ernest.

- Algernon is romantically drawn to Cecily as soon as he meets her.

- Cecily tells Algernon that Jack plans to send him to Australia. Algernon thinks Cecily should help him mend his ways instead. Cecily says she doesn't have time, so Algernon says he will reform himself.

- Cecily and Algernon leave the garden to go inside for something to eat. When Miss Prism and Dr Chasuble return, they wonder where Cecily has gone.

A. REVIEWING

1. Why do you think Cecily does not enjoy learning German?
2. What are your first impressions of Miss Prism?
3. Do you like Cecily Cardew so far? Why or why not?
4. Why do you think Algernon was disappointed to find Jack was not there?
5. Is there any evidence that Cecily and Algernon like each other?

B. EXPLORING

Becoming a Dramaturg

A dramaturg is a person who helps with the staging of a play by making sure it is properly researched, clearly explained and correctly produced.

Imagine you are the dramaturg for a production of *The Importance of Being Earnest*. Your director has asked you to do the following two things:

1. Research how young upper-class people were educated in Victorian society. This will help your director better understand the characters of Miss Prism and Cecily.

2. Draw and label a sketch of how you think the stage should look at the start of Act 2. Think about the backdrop and the props that will be needed.

Turn to **page 27** of your portfolio to complete these activities.

C. ORAL LANGUAGE

1. Discussing Food as a Symbol

Pair Activity

A **symbol** is an object, person or situation that represents (stands for) something else. Symbols are another way for a writer to explore an idea.

Food is an important symbol in *The Importance of Being Earnest*. Algernon, especially, is often seen eating or talking about food.

a. In pairs, try to remember the different times Algernon has mentioned or eaten food in the play so far.

b. With your partner, discuss what you think food symbolises about Algernon's character. What does his obsession with eating tell us about the type of person he is?

c. Can you identify any other symbols in the play? Share your suggestions with the class.

2. Talking About Dramatic Irony

Group Activity

Dramatic irony occurs when the audience or certain characters know something that other characters do not know.

For example, in this part of Act 2 the audience knows that the man claiming to be Ernest is actually Algernon. However, Cecily believes he is really Jack's younger brother.

In groups, discuss:

a. Why you think Wilde uses the device of dramatic irony in the play.

b. Any other examples of dramatic irony that you can think of in *The Importance of Being Earnest*.

ACT 2, PART 2

In this part of the act you will:

- Explore the **humour** in the play by analysing the actions of Cecily and Algernon.
- Witness how hard it is for Jack and Algernon to keep up their **lies**.
- See Algernon's love for Cecily revealed in a **soliloquy**.

[*Enter JACK slowly from the back of the garden. He is dressed in the deepest mourning, with crape hatband and black gloves*]

MISS PRISM
Mr Worthing!

CHASUBLE
Mr Worthing?

MISS PRISM
This is indeed a surprise. We did not look for you till Monday afternoon.

JACK
[*Shakes MISS PRISM's hand in a tragic manner*] I have returned sooner than I expected. Dr Chasuble, I hope you are well?

CHASUBLE
Dear Mr Worthing, I trust this garb[1] of woe does not betoken[2] some terrible calamity[3]?

JACK
My brother.

MISS PRISM
More shameful debts and extravagance?

CHASUBLE
Still leading his life of pleasure?

1. clothing
2. mean
3. tragedy

JACK

 [*Shaking his head*] Dead!

CHASUBLE

Your brother Ernest dead?

JACK

Quite dead.

MISS PRISM

What a lesson for him! I trust he will profit by it.

CHASUBLE

Mr Worthing, I offer you my sincere condolence[4]. You have at least the consolation[5] of knowing that you are always the most generous and forgiving of brothers.

4. sympathy

5. comfort

JACK

Poor Ernest! He had many faults, but it is a sad, sad blow.

CHASUBLE

Very sad indeed. Were you with him at the end?

JACK

No. He died abroad; in Paris, in fact. I had a telegram last night from the manager of the Grand Hotel.

CHASUBLE

Was the cause of death mentioned?

JACK

A severe chill, it seems.

MISS PRISM

As a man sows, so shall he reap.

CHASUBLE

[*Raising his hand*] Charity, dear Miss Prism, charity! None of us are perfect. I myself am peculiarly susceptible[6] to draughts. Will the interment[7] take place here?

JACK

No. He seems to have expressed a desire to be buried in Paris.

CHASUBLE

In Paris! [*Shakes his head*] I fear that hardly points to any very serious state of mind at the last. You would no doubt wish me to make some slight allusion[8] to this tragic domestic affliction[9] next Sunday. [*JACK presses his hand convulsively*[10]] My sermon on the meaning of the manna in the wilderness[11] can be adapted to almost any occasion, joyful, or, as in the present case, distressing. [*All sigh*] I have preached it at harvest celebrations, christenings, confirmations, on days of humiliation and festal[12] days. The last time I delivered it was in the Cathedral, as a charity sermon on behalf of the Society for the Prevention of Discontent among the Upper Orders. The Bishop, who was present, was much struck by some of the analogies[13] I drew.

6. likely to be harmed by
7. burial

8. reference
9. trouble
10. frantically
11. A Biblical reference to Exodus 16, in which food was supplied to the Israelites in the wilderness in a miracle.

12. celebration

13. comparisons

JACK

Ah! that reminds me, you mentioned christenings I think, Dr Chasuble? I suppose you know how to christen all right? [*DR CHASUBLE looks astounded*] I mean, of course, you are continually christening, aren't you?

MISS PRISM

It is, I regret to say, one of the Rector's most constant duties in this parish. I have often spoken to the poorer classes on the subject. But they don't seem to know what thrift is.

CHASUBLE

But is there any particular infant in whom you are interested, Mr Worthing? Your brother was, I believe, unmarried, was he not?

JACK

Oh yes.

MISS PRISM

[*Bitterly*] People who live entirely for pleasure usually are.

JACK

But it is not for any child, dear Doctor. I am very fond of children. No! the fact is, I would like to be christened myself, this afternoon, if you have nothing better to do.

CHASUBLE

But surely, Mr Worthing, you have been christened already?

JACK

I don't remember anything about it.

CHASUBLE

But have you any grave doubts on the subject?

JACK

I certainly intend to have. Of course I don't know if the thing would bother you in any way, or if you think I am a little too old now.

CHASUBLE

Not at all. The sprinkling, and, indeed, the immersion[14] of adults is a perfectly canonical practice[15].

JACK

Immersion!

CHASUBLE

You need have no apprehensions[16]. Sprinkling is all that is necessary, or indeed I think advisable. Our weather is so changeable. At what hour would you wish the ceremony performed?

JACK

Oh, I might trot round about five if that would suit you.

CHASUBLE

Perfectly, perfectly! In fact I have two similar ceremonies to perform at that time. A case of twins that occurred recently in one of the outlying cottages on your own estate. Poor Jenkins the carter[17], a most hard-working man.

JACK

Oh! I don't see much fun in being christened along with other babies. It would be childish. Would half-past five do?

14. baptism by placing a person's whole body in water
15. church law

16. fear

17. person who drives a cart

CHASUBLE

Admirably! Admirably! [*Takes out watch*] And now, dear Mr Worthing, I will not intrude any longer into a house of sorrow. I would merely beg you not to be too much bowed down by grief. What seem to us bitter trials are often blessings in disguise.

MISS PRISM

This seems to me a blessing of an extremely obvious kind.

[*Enter CECILY from the house*]

CECILY

Uncle Jack! Oh, I am pleased to see you back. But what horrid clothes you have got on! Do go and change them.

MISS PRISM

Cecily!

CHASUBLE

My child! my child.

[*CECILY goes towards JACK; he kisses her brow in a melancholy*[18] *manner*]

18. sad

CECILY

What is the matter, Uncle Jack? Do look happy! You look as if you had toothache, and I have got such a surprise for you. Who do you think is in the dining-room? Your brother!

JACK

Who?

CECILY

Your brother Ernest. He arrived about half an hour ago.

JACK

What nonsense! I haven't got a brother.

CECILY

Oh, don't say that. However badly he may have behaved to you in the past he is still your brother. You couldn't be so heartless as to disown him. I'll tell him to come out. And you will shake hands with him, won't you, Uncle Jack? [*Runs back into the house*]

CHASUBLE

These are very joyful tidings.

MISS PRISM

19. accepted

After we had all been resigned to[19] his loss, his sudden return seems to me peculiarly distressing.

JACK

My brother is in the dining-room? I don't know what it all means. I think it is perfectly absurd.

[*Enter ALGERNON and CECILY hand in hand. They come slowly up to JACK*]

JACK

Good heavens! [*Motions ALGERNON away*]

ALGERNON

Brother John, I have come down from town to tell you that I am very sorry for all the trouble I have given you, and that I intend to lead a better life in the future. [*JACK glares at him and does not take his hand*]

CECILY

Uncle Jack, you are not going to refuse your own brother's hand?

JACK

Nothing will induce me to take his hand. I think his coming down here disgraceful. He knows perfectly well why.

CECILY

Uncle Jack, do be nice. There is some good in everyone. Ernest has just been telling me about his poor invalid friend Mr Bunbury whom he goes to visit so often. And surely there must be much good in one who is kind to an invalid, and leaves the pleasures of London to sit by a bed of pain.

JACK

Oh! He has been talking about Bunbury, has he?

CECILY

Yes, he has told me all about poor Mr Bunbury, and his terrible state of health.

JACK

Bunbury! Well, I won't have him talk to you about Bunbury or about anything else. It is enough to drive one perfectly frantic.

ALGERNON

Of course I admit that the faults were all on my side. But I must say that I think that Brother John's coldness to me is peculiarly painful. I expected a more enthusiastic welcome, especially considering it is the first time I have come here.

CECILY

Uncle Jack, if you don't shake hands with Ernest I will never forgive you.

JACK

Never forgive me?

CECILY

Never, never, never!

JACK

Well, this is the last time I shall ever do it. [*Shakes with ALGERNON and glares*]

CHASUBLE

It's pleasant, is it not, to see so perfect a reconciliation[20]? I think we might leave the two brothers together.

MISS PRISM

Cecily, you will come with us.

CECILY

Certainly, Miss Prism. My little task of reconciliation is over.

CHASUBLE

You have done a beautiful action today, dear child.

MISS PRISM

We must not be premature[21] in our judgments.

CECILY

I feel very happy. [*They all go off except JACK and ALGERNON*]

JACK

You young scoundrel, Algy, you must get out of this place as soon as possible. I don't allow any Bunburying here.

[*Enter MERRIMAN*]

MERRIMAN

I have put Mr Ernest's things in the room next to yours, sir. I suppose that is all right?

JACK

What?

MERRIMAN

Mr Ernest's luggage, sir. I have unpacked it and put it in the room next to your own.

JACK

His luggage?

MERRIMAN

Yes, sir. Three portmanteaus[22], a dressing-case, two hat-boxes, and a large luncheon-basket.

ALGERNON

I am afraid I can't stay more than a week this time.

22. large travelling bags

JACK

Merriman, order the dog-cart[23] at once. Mr Ernest has been suddenly called back to town.

23. a carriage with back-to-back seats

MERRIMAN

Yes, sir. [*Goes back into the house*]

ALGERNON

What a fearful liar you are, Jack. I have not been called back to town at all.

JACK

Yes, you have.

ALGERNON

I haven't heard anyone call me.

JACK

Your duty as a gentleman calls you back.

ALGERNON

My duty as a gentleman has never interfered with my pleasures in the smallest degree.

JACK

I can quite understand that.

ALGERNON

Well, Cecily is a darling.

JACK

You are not to talk of Miss Cardew like that. I don't like it.

ALGERNON

Well, I don't like your clothes. You look perfectly ridiculous in them. Why on earth don't you go up and change? It is perfectly childish to be in deep mourning for a man who is actually staying for a whole week with you in your house as a guest. I call it grotesque[24].

JACK

You are certainly not staying with me for a whole week as a guest or anything else. You have got to leave . . . by the four-five train.

ALGERNON

I certainly won't leave you so long as you are in mourning. It would be most unfriendly. If I were in mourning you would stay with me, I suppose. I should think it very unkind if you didn't.

JACK

Well, will you go if I change my clothes?

ALGERNON

Yes, if you are not too long. I never saw anybody take so long to dress, and with such little result.

JACK

Well, at any rate, that is better than being always over-dressed as you are.

ALGERNON

If I am occasionally a little over-dressed, I make up for it by being always immensely over-educated.

24. twisted/ridiculous

JACK

Your vanity[25] is ridiculous, your conduct[26] an outrage, and your presence in my garden utterly absurd. However, you have got to catch the four-five, and I hope you will have a pleasant journey back to town. This Bunburying, as you call it, has not been a great success for you. [*Goes into the house*]

ALGERNON

I think it has been a great success. I'm in love with Cecily, and that is everything.

[*Enter CECILY at the back of the garden. She picks up the can and begins to water the flowers*]

But I must see her before I go, and make arrangements for another Bunbury. Ah, there she is.

CECILY

Oh, I merely came back to water the roses. I thought you were with Uncle Jack.

ALGERNON

He's gone to order the dog-cart for me.

CECILY

Oh, is he going to take you for a nice drive?

ALGERNON

He's going to send me away.

CECILY

Then have we got to part?

ALGERNON

I am afraid so. It's a very painful parting.

CECILY

It is always painful to part from people whom one has known for a very brief space of time. The absence of old friends one can endure with equanimity[27]. But even a momentary separation from anyone to whom one has just been introduced is almost unbearable.

25. self-importance
26. behaviour

27. calmness

ALGERNON

Thank you.

[*Enter MERRIMAN*]

MERRIMAN

The dog-cart is at the door, sir.

[*ALGERNON looks appealingly at CECILY*]

CECILY

It can wait, Merriman . . . for . . . five minutes.

MERRIMAN

Yes, miss. [*Exit MERRIMAN*]

ALGERNON

I hope, Cecily, I shall not offend you if I state quite frankly and openly that you seem to me to be in every way the visible personification[28] of absolute perfection.

CECILY

I think your frankness does you great credit, Ernest. If you will allow me, I will copy your remarks into my diary. [*Goes over to table and begins writing in diary*]

ALGERNON

Do you really keep a diary? I'd give anything to look at it. May I?

CECILY

Oh no. [*Puts her hand over it*] You see, it is simply a very young girl's record of her own thoughts and impressions, and consequently[29] meant for publication. When it appears in volume form I hope you will order a copy. But pray, Ernest, don't stop. I delight in taking down from dictation[30]. I have reached 'absolute perfection'. You can go on. I am quite ready for more.

ALGERNON

[*Somewhat taken aback*] Ahem! Ahem!

28. representation/example

29. as a result/therefore

30. spoken words

CECILY

Oh, don't cough, Ernest. When one is dictating one should speak fluently and not cough. Besides, I don't know how to spell a cough. [*Writes as ALGERNON speaks*]

ALGERNON

[*Speaking very rapidly*] Cecily, ever since I first looked upon your wonderful and incomparable beauty, I have dared to love you wildly, passionately, devotedly, hopelessly.

CECILY

I don't think that you should tell me that you love me wildly, passionately, devotedly, hopelessly. Hopelessly doesn't seem to make much sense, does it?

ALGERNON

Cecily!

[*Enter MERRIMAN*]

MERRIMAN

The dog-cart is waiting, sir.

ALGERNON

Tell it to come round next week, at the same hour.

MERRIMAN

[*Looks at CECILY, who makes no sign*] Yes, sir.

[*MERRIMAN retires*]

CECILY

Uncle Jack would be very much annoyed if he knew you were staying on till next week, at the same hour.

ALGERNON

Oh, I don't care about Jack. I don't care for anybody in the whole world but you. I love you, Cecily. You will marry me, won't you?

CECILY

You silly boy! Of course. Why, we have been engaged for the last three months.

ALGERNON

For the last three months?

CECILY

Yes, it will be exactly three months on Thursday.

ALGERNON

But how did we become engaged?

CECILY

Well, ever since dear Uncle Jack first confessed to us that he had a younger brother who was very wicked and bad, you of course have formed the chief topic of conversation between myself and Miss Prism. And of course a man who is much talked about is always very attractive. One feels there must be something in him, after all. I daresay it was foolish of me, but I fell in love with you, Ernest.

ALGERNON

Darling! And when was the engagement actually settled?

CECILY

On the 14th of February last. Worn out by your entire ignorance of my existence, I determined to end the matter one way or the other, and after a long struggle with myself I accepted you under this dear old tree here. The next day I bought this little ring in your name, and this is the little bangle with the true lovers' knot I promised you always to wear.

ALGERNON

Did I give you this? It's very pretty, isn't it?

CECILY

Yes, you've wonderfully good taste, Ernest. It's the excuse I've always given for your leading such a bad life. And this is the box in which I keep all your dear letters. [*Kneels at table, opens box, and produces letters tied up with blue ribbon*]

ALGERNON

My letters! But, my own sweet Cecily, I have never written you any letters.

CECILY

You need hardly remind me of that, Ernest. I remember only too well that I was forced to write your letters for you. I wrote always three times a week, and sometimes oftener.

ALGERNON

Oh, do let me read them, Cecily!

CECILY

Oh, I couldn't possibly. They would make you far too conceited[31]. [*Replaces box*] The three you wrote me after I had broken off the engagement are so beautiful, and so badly spelled, that even now I can hardly read them without crying a little.

ALGERNON

But was our engagement ever broken off?

CECILY

Of course it was. On the 22nd of last March. You can see the entry if you like. [*Shows diary*] 'Today I broke off my engagement with Ernest. I feel it is better to do so. The weather still continues charming.'

ALGERNON

But why on earth did you break it off? What had I done? I had done nothing at all. Cecily, I am very much hurt indeed to hear you broke it off. Particularly when the weather was so charming.

31. vain

CECILY

 It would hardly have been a really serious engagement if it hadn't been broken off at least once. But I forgave you before the week was out.

ALGERNON

[*Crossing to her, and kneeling*] What a perfect angel you are, Cecily.

CECILY

You dear romantic boy. [*He kisses her, she puts her fingers through his hair*] I hope your hair curls naturally, does it?

ALGERNON

Yes, darling, with a little help from others.

CECILY

I am so glad.

ALGERNON

You'll never break off our engagement again, Cecily?

CECILY

I don't think I could break it off now that I have actually met you.
Besides, of course, there is the question of your name.

ALGERNON

[*Nervously*] —Yes, of course.

CECILY

You must not laugh at me, darling, but it had always been a
girlish dream of mine to love someone whose name was Ernest.
[*ALGERNON rises, CECILY also*] There is something in that name
that seems to inspire absolute confidence. I pity any poor married
woman whose husband is not called Ernest.

ALGERNON

But, my dear child, do you mean to say you could not love me if I
had some other name?

CECILY

But what name?

ALGERNON

Oh, any name you like—Algernon—for instance . . .

CECILY

But I don't like the name of Algernon.

ALGERNON

Well, my own dear, sweet, loving little darling, I really can't see why
you should object to the name of Algernon. It is not at all a bad
name. In fact, it is rather an aristocratic[32] name. Half of the chaps
who get into the Bankruptcy Court are called Algernon.
But seriously, Cecily . . . [*Moving to her*] . . . if my name was Algy,
couldn't you love me?

32. upper-class/noble

CECILY

[*Rising*] I might respect you, Ernest, I might admire your character,
but I fear that I should not be able to give you my undivided
attention.

ALGERNON

Ahem! Cecily! [*Picking up hat*] Your Rector here is, I suppose, thoroughly experienced in the practice of all the rites and ceremonials of the Church?

CECILY

Oh, yes. Dr Chasuble is a most learned man. He has never written a single book, so you can imagine how much he knows.

ALGERNON

I must see him at once on a most important christening—I mean on most important business.

CECILY

Oh!

ALGERNON

I shan't be away more than half an hour.

CECILY

Considering that we have been engaged since February the 14th, and that I only met you today for the first time, I think it is rather hard that you should leave me for so long a period as half an hour. Couldn't you make it twenty minutes?

ALGERNON

I'll be back in no time.
[*Kisses her and rushes down the garden*]

CECILY

What an impetuous[33] boy he is! I like his hair so much. I must enter his proposal in my diary.

33. impulsive

ACTION SUMMARY ACT 2, PART 2

- Jack returns to his country home dressed in black and tells Miss Prism and Dr Chasuble that his brother Ernest has died in Paris.
- Jack makes arrangements to be christened by Dr Chasuble, in order to take the name Ernest.
- Cecily tells Jack that his brother Ernest is in the dining room.
- Jack is angry that the person pretending to be Ernest is Algernon.
- Cecily makes Jack and Algernon shake hands. Miss Prism, Dr Chasuble and Cecily leave the 'brothers' alone to talk.
- Algernon tells Jack that he will leave if Jack changes his clothes. While Jack is gone, Algernon reveals that he loves Cecily.
- Algernon asks Cecily to marry him. Cecily tells him that they are already engaged as she proposed to herself, on Ernest's behalf, in her diary.
- Cecily tells Algernon how important it is that her husband is called Ernest.
- Algernon rushes off to find Dr Chasuble so that he can also arrange to be christened Ernest.
- Cecily writes Algernon's proposal into her diary.

A. REVIEWING

1. What happens when Cecily tells Jack that his brother Ernest is in the dining room?
2. How does Jack behave with Algernon?
3. Compare Lane from Act 1 with Merriman from Act 2. Which servant character do you like most? Why?
4. What is odd about the engagement between Algernon and Cecily?
5. What do Jack and Algernon's plans to be christened tell us about their attitude to religion?

B. EXPLORING

1. Cecily's Diary

In this part of Act 2 we find out that Cecily proposed to herself on behalf of Ernest on Valentine's day.

Go to **page 29** of your portfolio to write Cecily's diary entry for that day. Include the details of the conversation you think Cecily had with herself under the tree.

2. Algernon and Cecily's Witty Words

There is a lot of humour in this part of the play, as the lies and fantasies build up. The conversation between Algernon and Cecily is especially humorous as a result.

Choose two quotes from each character that you found humorous and fill in the grid on **page 31** of your portfolio.

C. ORAL LANGUAGE

Taking Sides

Pair Activity

Imagine you're a friend of Algernon and Jack's. Whose side would you take in this situation and why?

Discuss it in pairs, then explain your view to the class. After every pair has shared their view, have a show of hands to see who the class sides with most.

D. CREATING

1. Making Up Portmanteaus

When Algernon arrives at the Manor House he has three portmanteaus.

The word 'portmanteau' has two meanings:

- A large case that opens in two sections.
- A word that is made by combining two other words together. For example, the words 'friend' and 'enemy' are combined to create the word 'frenemy' and the words 'breakfast' and 'lunch' are combined to make the word 'brunch'.

Go to **page 32** of your portfolio and make up a portmanteau to describe each character so far. Think of two words that describe the character, then join them together to make your portmanteau. For example, we might call Algernon a 'chibber', because he is both charming and a fibber!

2. Create Your Own Alter Ego

An alter ego is a second self that allows a person to live a double life. Both Jack and Algernon pretend to be the fictional character Ernest. As Ernest, they can say and do things that they would not as their 'real' selves.

Turn to **page 33** of your portfolio to create your own alter ego.

ACT 2, PART 3

In this part of the act you will:

- Find out more about **Cecily** and **Gwendolen**.
- Identify moments when Wilde **mirrors** characters, dialogue and events.

[*Enter MERRIMAN*]

MERRIMAN

A Miss Fairfax has just called to see Mr Worthing. On very important business, Miss Fairfax states.

CECILY

Isn't Mr Worthing in his library?

MERRIMAN

Mr Worthing went over in the direction of the Rectory some time ago.

CECILY

Pray ask the lady to come out here; Mr Worthing is sure to be back soon. And you can bring tea.

MERRIMAN

Yes, Miss. [*Goes out*]

CECILY

Miss Fairfax! I suppose one of the many good elderly women who are associated with Uncle Jack in some of his philanthropic[1] work in London. I don't quite like women who are interested in philanthropic work. I think it is so forward of them.

[*Enter MERRIMAN*]

MERRIMAN

Miss Fairfax.

1. charitable

[*Enter GWENDOLEN*]

[*Exit MERRIMAN*]

CECILY

[*Advancing to meet her*] Pray let me introduce myself to you. My name is Cecily Cardew.

GWENDOLEN

Cecily Cardew? [*Moving to her and shaking hands*] What a very sweet name! Something tells me that we are going to be great friends. I like you already more than I can say. My first impressions of people are never wrong.

CECILY

How nice of you to like me so much after we have known each other such a comparatively short time. Pray sit down.

GWENDOLEN

[*Still standing up*] I may call you Cecily, may I not?

CECILY

With pleasure!

GWENDOLEN

And you will always call me Gwendolen, won't you?

CECILY

If you wish.

GWENDOLEN

Then that is all quite settled, is it not?

CECILY

I hope so. [*A pause. They both sit down together*]

GWENDOLEN

Perhaps this might be a favourable opportunity for my mentioning who I am. My father is Lord Bracknell. You have never heard of papa, I suppose?

CECILY

I don't think so.

GWENDOLEN

Outside the family circle, papa, I am glad to say, is entirely unknown. I think that is quite as it should be. The home seems to me to be the proper sphere for the man. And certainly once a man begins to neglect his domestic duties he becomes painfully effeminate[2], does he not? And I don't like that. It makes men so very attractive. Cecily, mamma, whose views on education are remarkably strict, has brought me up to be extremely short-sighted; it is part of her system; so do you mind my looking at you through my glasses?

CECILY

Oh! not at all, Gwendolen. I am very fond of being looked at.

GWENDOLEN

[*After examining Cecily carefully through a lorgnette*[3]] You are here on a short visit, I suppose.

2. having qualities usually linked to a woman/unmanly

3. opera-style glasses with a single handle at the side

CECILY

Oh no! I live here.

GWENDOLEN

[*Severely*] Really? Your mother, no doubt, or some female relative of advanced years, resides here also?

CECILY

Oh no! I have no mother, nor, in fact, any relations.

GWENDOLEN

Indeed?

CECILY

My dear guardian, with the assistance of Miss Prism, has the arduous[4] task of looking after me.

GWENDOLEN

Your guardian?

CECILY

Yes, I am Mr Worthing's ward[5].

GWENDOLEN

Oh! It is strange he never mentioned to me that he had a ward. How secretive of him! He grows more interesting hourly. I am not sure, however, that the news inspires me with feelings of unmixed delight. [*Rising and going to her*] I am very fond of you, Cecily; I have liked you ever since I met you! But I am bound to state that now that I know that you are Mr Worthing's ward, I cannot help expressing a wish you were—well just a little older than you seem to be—and not quite so very alluring[6] in appearance. In fact, if I may speak candidly[7]—

CECILY

Pray do! I think that whenever one has anything unpleasant to say, one should always be quite candid.

GWENDOLEN

Well, to speak with perfect candour[8], Cecily, I wish that you were fully forty-two, and more than usually plain for your age.

4. difficult

5. someone placed under the protection of a legal guardian

6. attractive

7. truthfully

8. honesty

Ernest has a strong upright nature. He is the very soul of truth and honour. Disloyalty would be as impossible to him as deception. But even men of the noblest possible moral character are extremely susceptible[9] to the influence of the physical charms of others. Modern, no less than Ancient History, supplies us with many most painful examples of what I refer to. If it were not so, indeed, History would be quite unreadable.

9. sensitive/vulnerable

CECILY

I beg your pardon, Gwendolen, did you say Ernest?

GWENDOLEN

Yes.

CECILY

Oh, but it is not Mr Ernest Worthing who is my guardian. It is his brother—his elder brother.

GWENDOLEN

[*Sitting down again*] Ernest never mentioned to me that he had a brother.

CECILY

I am sorry to say they have not been on good terms for a long time.

GWENDOLEN

Ah! that accounts for it. And now that I think of it I have never heard any man mention his brother. The subject seems distasteful to most men. Cecily, you have lifted a load from my mind. I was growing almost anxious. It would have been terrible if any cloud had come across a friendship like ours, would it not? Of course you are quite, quite sure that it is not Mr Ernest Worthing who is your guardian?

CECILY

Quite sure. [*A pause*] In fact, I am going to be his.

GWENDOLEN

[*Enquiringly*] I beg your pardon?

CECILY

[*Rather shy and confidingly*] Dearest Gwendolen, there is no reason why I should make a secret of it to you. Our little county newspaper

is sure to chronicle the fact next week. Mr Ernest Worthing and I are engaged to be married.

GWENDOLEN

[*Quite politely, rising*] My darling Cecily, I think there must be some slight error. Mr Ernest Worthing is engaged to me. The announcement will appear in the *Morning Post* on Saturday at the latest.

CECILY

[*Very politely, rising*] I am afraid you must be under some misconception[10]. Ernest proposed to me exactly ten minutes ago. [*Shows diary*]

10. misunderstanding

GWENDOLEN

[*Examines diary through her lorgnettte carefully*] It is very curious, for he asked me to be his wife yesterday afternoon at 5.30. If you would care to verify the incident, pray do so. [*Produces diary of her own*] I never travel without my diary. One should always have something sensational to read in the train. I am so sorry, dear Cecily, if it is any disappointment to you, but I am afraid *I* have the prior claim.

CECILY

It would distress me more than I can tell you, dear Gwendolen, if it caused you any mental or physical anguish, but I feel bound to point out that since Ernest proposed to you he clearly has changed his mind.

GWENDOLEN

[*Meditatively*[11]] If the poor fellow has been entrapped into any foolish promise I shall consider it my duty to rescue him at once, and with a firm hand.

11. thoughtfully

CECILY

[*Thoughtfully and sadly*] Whatever unfortunate entanglement[12] my dear boy may have got into, I will never reproach[13] him with it after we are married.

12. mix-up

13. disapprove of

GWENDOLEN

Do you allude to[14] me, Miss Cardew, as an entanglement? You are presumptuous[15]. On an occasion of this kind it becomes more than a moral duty to speak one's mind. It becomes a pleasure.

14. suggest/hint at

15. overconfident/forward

CECILY

Do you suggest, Miss Fairfax, that I entrapped Ernest into an engagement? How dare you? This is no time for wearing the shallow mask of manners. When I see a spade I call it a spade.

GWENDOLEN

[*Satirically*[16]] I am glad to say that I have never seen a spade. It is obvious that our social spheres have been widely different.

16. mockingly

ACT 2, PART 3

17. reply

18. become annoyed

19. nearby

[*Enter MERRIMAN, followed by the footman. He carries a salver, table cloth, and plate stand. CECILY is about to retort[17]. The presence of the servants exercises a restraining influence, under which both girls chafe[18]*]

MERRIMAN

Shall I lay tea here as usual, Miss?

CECILY

[*Sternly, in a calm voice*] Yes, as usual.

[*MERRIMAN begins to clear table and lay cloth. A long pause. CECILY and GWENDOLEN glare at each other*]

GWENDOLEN

Are there many interesting walks in the vicinity[19], Miss Cardew?

CECILY

Oh! yes! a great many. From the top of one of the hills quite close one can see five counties.

GWENDOLEN

Five counties! I don't think I should like that; I hate crowds.

CECILY

[*Sweetly*] I suppose that is why you live in town? [*GWENDOLEN bites her lip, and beats her foot nervously with her parasol*]

GWENDOLEN

[*Looking round*] Quite a well-kept garden this is, Miss Cardew.

CECILY

So glad you like it, Miss Fairfax.

GWENDOLEN

I had no idea there were any flowers in the country.

CECILY

Oh, flowers are as common here, Miss Fairfax, as people are in London.

90 THE IMPORTANCE OF BEING EARNEST

GWENDOLEN

Personally I cannot understand how anybody manages to exist in the country, if anybody who is anybody does. The country always bores me to death.

CECILY

Ah! This is what the newspapers call agricultural[20] depression, is it not? I believe the aristocracy are suffering very much from it just at present. It is almost an epidemic[21] amongst them, I have been told. May I offer you some tea, Miss Fairfax?

20. relating to farming

21. outbreak

GWENDOLEN

[*With elaborate politeness*] Thank you. [*Aside*] Detestable girl! But I require tea!

CECILY

[*Sweetly*] Sugar?

GWENDOLEN

[*Superciliously*[22]] No, thank you. Sugar is not fashionable any more. [*CECILY looks angrily at her, takes up the tongs and puts four lumps of sugar into the cup*]

22. patronisingly/arrogantly

CECILY

[*Severely*] Cake or bread and butter?

GWENDOLEN

 [*In a bored manner*] Bread and butter, please. Cake is rarely seen at the best houses nowadays.

CECILY

[*Cuts a very large slice of cake and puts it on the tray*] Hand that to Miss Fairfax.

[*MERRIMAN does so, and goes out with footman. GWENDOLEN drinks the tea and makes a grimace[23]. Puts down cup at once, reaches out her hand to the bread and butter, looks at it, and finds it is cake. Rises in indignation[24]*]

GWENDOLEN

You have filled my tea with lumps of sugar, and though I asked most distinctly for bread and butter, you have given me cake. I am known for the gentleness of my disposition[25], and the extraordinary sweetness of my nature, but I warn you, Miss Cardew, you may go too far.

CECILY

[*Rising*] To save my poor, innocent, trusting boy from the machinations[26] of any other girl there are no lengths to which I would not go.

GWENDOLEN

From the moment I saw you I distrusted you. I felt that you were false and deceitful. I am never deceived in such matters. My first impressions of people are invariably right.

CECILY

It seems to me, Miss Fairfax, that I am trespassing on your valuable time. No doubt you have many other calls of a similar character to make in the neighbourhood.

[Enter *JACK*]

GWENDOLEN

[*Catching sight of him*] Ernest! My own Ernest!

23. look of disgust

24. anger

25. character

26. scheming

JACK

Gwendolen! Darling! [*Offers to kiss her*]

GWENDOLEN

[*Drawing back*] A moment! May I ask if you are engaged to be married to this young lady? [*Points to CECILY*]

JACK

[*Laughing*] To dear little Cecily! Of course not! What could have put such an idea into your pretty little head?

GWENDOLEN

Thank you. You may! [*Offers her cheek*]

CECILY

[*Very sweetly*] I knew there must be some misunderstanding, Miss Fairfax. The gentleman whose arm is at present round your waist is my guardian, Mr John Worthing.

GWENDOLEN

I beg your pardon?

CECILY

This is Uncle Jack.

GWENDOLEN

[*Receding*] Jack! Oh!

[*Enter ALGERNON*]

CECILY

Here is Ernest.

ALGERNON

[*Goes straight over to CECILY without noticing anyone else*] My own love! [*Offers to kiss her*]

CECILY

[*Drawing back*] A moment, Ernest! May I ask you—are you engaged to be married to this young lady?

ALGERNON

[*Looking round*] To what young lady? Good heavens! Gwendolen!

CECILY

Yes! to good heavens, Gwendolen, I mean to Gwendolen.

ALGERNON

[*Laughing*] Of course not! What could have put such an idea into your pretty little head?

CECILY

Thank you. [*Presenting her cheek to be kissed*] You may. [*ALGERNON kisses her*]

GWENDOLEN

I felt there was some slight error, Miss Cardew. The gentleman who is now embracing you is my cousin, Mr Algernon Moncrieff.

CECILY

[*Breaking away from ALGERNON*] Algernon Moncrieff! Oh! [*The two girls move towards each other and put their arms round each other's waists as if for protection*]

CECILY

Are you called Algernon?

ALGERNON

I cannot deny it.

CECILY

Oh!

GWENDOLEN

Is your name really John?

JACK

[*Standing rather proudly*] I could deny it if I liked. I could deny anything if I liked. But my name certainly is John. It has been John for years.

CECILY

[*To GWENDOLEN*] A gross deception has been practised on both of us.

GWENDOLEN

My poor wounded Cecily!

CECILY

My sweet wronged Gwendolen!

GWENDOLEN

[*Slowly and seriously*] You will call me sister, will you not? [*They embrace. JACK and ALGERNON groan and walk up and down*]

CECILY

[*Rather brightly*] There is just one question I would like to be allowed to ask my guardian.

GWENDOLEN

An admirable idea! Mr Worthing, there is just one question I would like to be permitted to put to you. Where is your brother Ernest? We are both engaged to be married to your brother Ernest, so it is a matter of some importance to us to know where your brother Ernest is at present.

JACK

[*Slowly and hesitatingly*] Gwendolen—Cecily—it is very painful for me to be forced to speak the truth. It is the first time in my life that I have ever been reduced to such a painful position, and I am really quite inexperienced in doing anything of the kind. However, I will tell you quite frankly that I have no brother Ernest. I have no brother at all. I never had a brother in my life, and I certainly have not the smallest intention of ever having one in the future.

CECILY

[*Surprised*] No brother at all?

JACK

[*Cheerily*] None!

GWENDOLEN

[*Severely*] Had you never a brother of any kind?

JACK

[*Pleasantly*] Never. Not even of any kind.

GWENDOLEN

I am afraid it is quite clear, Cecily, that neither of us is engaged to be married to anyone.

CECILY

It is not a very pleasant position for a young girl suddenly to find herself in. Is it?

GWENDOLEN

Let us go into the house. They will hardly venture to come after us there.

CECILY

No, men are so cowardly, aren't they?

[*They retire into the house with scornful looks*]

JACK

This ghastly state of things is what you call Bunburying, I suppose?

ALGERNON

Yes, and a perfectly wonderful Bunbury it is. The most wonderful Bunbury I have ever had in my life.

JACK

Well, you've no right whatsoever to Bunbury here.

ALGERNON

That is absurd. One has a right to Bunbury anywhere one chooses. Every serious Bunburyist knows that.

JACK

Serious Bunburyist! Good heavens!

ALGERNON

Well, one must be serious about something, if one wants to have any amusement in life. I happen to be serious about Bunburying. What on earth you are serious about I haven't got the remotest idea. About everything, I should fancy. You have such an absolutely trivial[27] nature.

27. foolish/superficial

JACK

Well, the only small satisfaction I have in the whole of this wretched[28] business is that your friend Bunbury is quite exploded[29]. You won't be able to run down to the country quite so often as you used to do, dear Algy. And a very good thing too.

28. terrible
29. shown to be false/exposed

ALGERNON

Your brother is a little off colour, isn't he, dear Jack? You won't be able to disappear to London quite so frequently as your wicked custom was. And not a bad thing either.

JACK

As for your conduct towards Miss Cardew, I must say that your taking in a sweet, simple, innocent girl like that is quite inexcusable. To say nothing of the fact that she is my ward.

ALGERNON

I can see no possible defence at all for your deceiving a brilliant, clever, thoroughly experienced young lady like Miss Fairfax. To say nothing of the fact that she is my cousin.

JACK

 I wanted to be engaged to Gwendolen, that is all. I love her.

ALGERNON

Well, I simply wanted to be engaged to Cecily. I adore her.

JACK

There is certainly no chance of your marrying Miss Cardew.

ALGERNON

I don't think there is much likelihood, Jack, of you and Miss Fairfax being united.

JACK

Well, that is no business of yours.

ALGERNON

If it was my business, I wouldn't talk about it. [*Begins to eat muffins*] It is very vulgar to talk about one's business. Only people like stockbrokers do that, and then merely at dinner parties.

JACK

How can you sit there, calmly eating muffins when we are in this horrible trouble, I can't make out. You seem to me to be perfectly heartless.

ALGERNON

Well, I can't eat muffins in an agitated[30] manner. The butter would probably get on my cuffs. One should always eat muffins quite calmly. It is the only way to eat them.

JACK

I say it's perfectly heartless your eating muffins at all, under the circumstances.

30. upset

ALGERNON

When I am in trouble, eating is the only thing that consoles me. Indeed, when I am in really great trouble, as anyone who knows me intimately[31] will tell you, I refuse everything except food and drink. At the present moment I am eating muffins because I am unhappy. Besides, I am particularly fond of muffins. [*Rising*]

JACK

[*Rising*] Well, that is no reason why you should eat them all in that greedy way. [*Takes muffins from ALGERNON*]

ALGERNON

[*Offering tea-cake*] I wish you would have tea-cake instead. I don't like tea-cake.

JACK

Good heavens! I suppose a man may eat his own muffins in his own garden.

31. well

ALGERNON

But you have just said it was perfectly heartless to eat muffins.

JACK

I said it was perfectly heartless of you, under the circumstances. That is a very different thing.

ALGERNON

That may be. But the muffins are the same. [*He seizes the muffin-dish from JACK*]

JACK

Algy, I wish to goodness you would go.

ALGERNON

You can't possibly ask me to go without having some dinner. It's absurd. I never go without my dinner. No one ever does, except vegetarians and people like that. Besides I have just made arrangements with Dr Chasuble to be christened at a quarter to six under the name of Ernest.

JACK

My dear fellow, the sooner you give up that nonsense the better. I made arrangements this morning with Dr Chasuble to be christened myself at 5.30, and I naturally will take the name of Ernest. Gwendolen would wish it. We can't both be christened Ernest. It's absurd. Besides, I have a perfect right to be christened if I like. There is no evidence at all that I have ever been christened by anybody. I should think it extremely probable I never was, and so does Dr Chasuble. It is entirely different in your case. You have been christened already.

ALGERNON

Yes, but I have not been christened for years.

JACK

Yes, but you have been christened. That is the important thing.

ALGERNON

Quite so. So I know my constitution[32] can stand it. If you are not quite sure about your ever having been christened, I must say I

32. character/health

think it rather dangerous your venturing on it now. It might make you very unwell. You can hardly have forgotten that someone very closely connected with you was very nearly carried off this week in Paris by a severe chill.

JACK

Yes, but you said yourself that a severe chill was not hereditary.

ALGERNON

It usen't to be, I know—but I daresay it is now. Science is always making wonderful improvements in things.

JACK

[*Picking up the muffin-dish*] Oh, that is nonsense; you are always talking nonsense.

ALGERNON

Jack, you are at the muffins again! I wish you wouldn't. There are only two left. [*Takes them*] I told you I was particularly fond of muffins.

JACK

But I hate tea-cake.

ALGERNON

Why on earth then do you allow tea-cake to be served up for your guests? What ideas you have of hospitality!

JACK

Algernon! I have already told you to go. I don't want you here. Why don't you go!

ALGERNON

I haven't quite finished my tea yet! and there is still one muffin left. [*JACK groans, and sinks into a chair. ALGERNON still continues eating*]

ACT ENDS

ACTION SUMMARY
ACT 2, PART 3

- Merriman tells Cecily that Gwendolen Fairfax has arrived at the Manor House looking for Mr Worthing.
- Gwendolen and Cecily meet.
- The ladies get along well until Cecily tells Gwendolen that she is Mr Worthing's ward.
- Gwendolen worries that Ernest may like the young, beautiful Cecily better than her.
- When Gwendolen mentions Ernest, Cecily is confused because Jack Worthing is her guardian and Ernest Worthing is the man she loves.
- Both women now believe that they are in love with a man called Ernest Worthing. They become more hostile (unfriendly) to one another. When the servants enter, Gwendolen and Cecily hide their annoyance.
- When Jack returns, Gwendolen calls him Ernest. Cecily realises that there has been a misunderstanding. Gwendolen is in love with Jack, not Algernon.
- Jack and Algernon reveal their true identities and admit that Ernest does not exist.
- Gwendolen and Cecily are angry and return to the house.
- Jack accuses Algernon of causing all this trouble by Bunburying.
- Both men still plan to be christened Ernest by Dr Chasuble.
- Jack asks Algernon to leave but Algernon replies that he has not yet finished his muffin.

A. REVIEWING

1. Do you think Cecily is a good role model for young women?
2. Gwendolen tells Cecily, 'From the moment I saw you I distrusted you.' Is this true?
3. Using evidence from the text, who do you think won the argument between Cecily and Gwendolen?
4. How would you describe the behavior of Jack and Algernon at the end of Act 2?

B. EXPLORING

Cecily and Gwendolen's Name Calling

Names are an important **motif** (repeated idea) in *The Importance of Being Earnest*.

In the last part of Act 2, the quickly changing relationship between Cecily and Gwendolen can be tracked based on how they address each other.

Go to **page 34** of your portfolio and write down examples of quotes in which the women use each other's first names or surnames. This will help you to follow the changes in how they feel about one another.

C. CREATING

Love Blooms

At the start of Act 2, Algernon asks Cecily for a flower to put in his jacket buttonhole. This is just one moment when the relationship between the couple 'blooms' in Act 2.

Find six more quotes that show the relationship between Algernon and Cecily growing in Act 2. Write them into the flower on **page 36** of your portfolio.

D. ORAL LANGUAGE

Mirroring

Pair Activity

In *The Importance of Being Earnest*, Oscar Wilde often mirrors characters, events and even dialogue. This technique is especially clear in part 3 of Act 2, where Cecily and Gwendolen and Jack and Algernon appear in pairs and often reflect each other's words and actions.

1. In your own pairs, read the following lines aloud (one person should read Jack's lines, the other Algernon's). Then discuss how the lines are the same and how they differ.

JACK: As for your conduct towards Miss Cardew, I must say that your taking in a sweet, simple, innocent girl like that is quite inexcusable. To say nothing of the fact that she is my ward.

ALGERNON: I can see no possible defence at all for your deceiving a brilliant, clever, thoroughly experienced young lady like Miss Fairfax. To say nothing of the fact that she is my cousin.

2. Why do you think Wilde uses this technique? Discuss with your partner and then share your opinions with the class.

E. REFLECTING

1. Character File

Turn to the Character File section of your portfolio and record your impressions of **Algernon**, **Jack**, **Gwendolen**, **Cecily**, **Miss Prism** and **Dr Chasuble** based on Act 2.

2. Mapping the Plot

Pair Activity

With your partner, turn to **page 5** of your portfolio and write ten sentences to sum up the main action in Act 2.

3. Act 2 Word Search

Go to **page 47** of your portfolio to complete the Act 2 word search.

OVERVIEW OF ACT 2

Cecily Cardew and Miss Prism

- Act 2 takes place at Jack's Manor House in the countryside. When the act opens, Jack's ward, Cecily Cardew, is having a lesson with her governess, Miss Prism.

- When Cecily tells Miss Prism that she wishes she could help Jack's brother Ernest, Miss Prism replies:

> *I am not in favour of this modern mania for turning bad people into good people at a moment's notice.*

Miss Prism's **moralistic** words take on further meaning in the context of a play in which people are adopting **new identities**.

- Miss Prism tells Cecily that she wrote a three-volume novel when she was young. This suggests that the governess is not quite as serious as she appears. Women reading, and especially writing, novels was considered silly and immodest by Victorian moral standards.

- Cecily is impressed that her governess has written a novel. She writes her own form of fiction in her diary.

- When Dr Chasuble arrives, he and Miss Prism flirt with each other, before leaving for a walk together. The suggestion is that those who tell other people how to behave, such as teachers and the clergy, are not always that well behaved themselves.

Jack returns to the Manor House

- Jack returns to the country and tells the **lie** that Ernest has died in Paris from a chill. When Algernon turns up pretending to be Ernest only moments later, nobody questions Jack's lies. Even when Jack blurts out the truth in his confusion, the other characters do not acknowledge his words:

> *What nonsense! I haven't got a brother.*

This shows how important an acceptance of the **absurd** (ridiculous) is in the play. Like the characters, we must go along with the things in the plot that don't seem realistic in order to enjoy the play's **comedy**.

Cecily and Algernon's romance

- When Ernest is announced, Cecily hopes that he is an exciting and wicked character:

> *I have never met any really wicked person before. I feel rather frightened. I am so afraid he will look just like everyone else.*

Again, Wilde is commenting on Victorian society's interest in immorality and wickedness, despite the importance they place on the appearance of **virtue** (goodness). And, as Jack and Algernon have shown, there is no way to tell who someone really is simply by looking at them.

- In the short time they have spent together, Algernon seems to have truly fallen in love with Cecily. He reveals this in a **soliloquy** when he is left alone:

> *I'm in love with Cecily, and that is everything.*

- Cecily tells Algernon that they have been engaged since 14 February, after she proposed to herself on his behalf. She even informs Algernon that the engagement was briefly broken on 22 March and that she has been writing love letters to herself from him. This continues the pattern of the play's characters leading **fictional lives**. It also makes fun of the shallow way that upper-class society thought of **marriage**.

- Cecily tells Algernon (whom she believes is called Ernest) that she could not marry a man named anything else:

> *I might respect you ... I might admire your character, but I fear that I should not be able to give you my undivided attention.*

Here, and throughout the play, Wilde is **satirising** the importance that upper-class Victorian society put on a person's name, rather than on their actions. In this play, being called Ernest is considered more important than actually being earnest (sincere).

By focusing on a Christian name rather than on a family name (which would indicate a person's social position and wealth), Wilde is saying that it is no more ridiculous to judge a person based on their first name than on their surname.

Learning more about the main characters

- There is a lot of **dramatic irony** in Act 2. The audience knows the true identities of Jack and Algernon, while Cecily and Gwendolen spend most of the act in the dark. This adds to the **comedy**.

- Act 2 tells us a lot about the personalities and **motivations** of the play's four central characters.

- Despite her youth and inventive mind, **Cecily** is is shown to be self-confident. She is capable of standing her ground against the older, city-living Gwendolen:

> *Do you suggest, Miss Fairfax, that I entrapped Ernest into an engagement? How dare you? This is no time for wearing the shallow mask of manners. When I see a spade I call it a spade.*

- **Gwendolen** is shown to be a fickle (changeable) character in Act 2. At first, she seems vulnerable and compares herself unfavourably to Cecily:

> *I cannot help expressing a wish you were—well, just a little older than you seem to be—and not quite so very alluring in appearance.*

When Gwendolen thinks that she and Cecily are competing for the same man, she becomes harsh in her treatment of Cecily. When the misunderstanding is cleared up, she is friendly to Cecily again:

> *You will call me sister, will you not?*

- Cecily and Gwendolen are both women who know exactly what they want: a husband called Ernest.

- **Jack** is forced to abandon his lies about Ernest and come clean to Gwendolen. Jack has always found telling lies easy, but falling in love with Gwendolen has changed that:

> *… it is very painful for me to be forced to speak the truth. It is the first time in my life that I have ever been reduced to such a painful position, and I am really quite inexperienced in doing anything of the kind. However, I will tell you quite frankly that I have no brother Ernest.*

- **Algernon** is shown to be a cool-headed character in Act 2. Jack panics when the truth is revealed to the ladies, but Algernon stays calm and eats muffins. When Jack tells him off for causing trouble, Algernon replies that it is 'The most wonderful Bunbury I have ever had in my life.' Jack accuses Algernon of being 'heartless'.

The role of the servants

- Gwendolen and Cecily cool their argument and pretend to be polite to one another as soon as Merriman and the footman enter the room. The 'shallow mask of manners' that Cecily and Gwendolen briefly threw off are fixed firmly in place in front of the staff. Both women know, without speaking, that they must play by the social rules. As the stage directions tell us, *'The presence of the servants exercises a restraining influence.'*

- Here, as elsewhere in the play, the servants are **foil characters** that show how superficial the aristocracy's manners really are. The staff's calm and dutiful conduct is in sharp contrast to their masters' foolish behaviour.

ACT 2 PROJECTS

Now that you have finished Act 2, you should reflect on what you have learned by doing *one* of the projects from options A and B below.

These projects will help you to prepare for the two Classroom Based Assessments (CBAs) you will complete as part of your Junior Cycle course.

Your first CBA will be an Oral Communication Task at the end of Second Year. Your second CBA will be a Collection of Texts Task in the middle of Third Year, which will involve selecting some of your written pieces.

A. Written Task

You have been asked to submit a presentation on 'The most memorable character in *The Importance of Being Earnest*'.

The judges have allowed three ways for entries to be submitted. Choose *one* and follow the success criteria for your choice on **page 37** of your portfolio.

1. Written presentation
2. Slideshow presentation
3. Multimedia presentation

Turn to **page 38** of your portfolio to plan and write your presentation.

When you have finished, complete the student reflection note on **page 42** of your portfolio.

B. Oral Communication Task

Pair Activity

1. In pairs, choose one character interaction, one oral language style and one location from the top hats. For example, Cecily and Gwendolen insult each other during a debate on the radio **or** Algernon and Jack poke fun at each other during sililoquies in private.

Cecily and Gwendolen insult each other

Algernon and Jack poke fun at each other

Miss Prism and Dr Chasuble flirt with each other

Soliloquy

Conversation

Debate

In private (perform each character's part)

Face to face

On the radio

2. Give your oral language task a title, plan it and perform it. Turn to **page 43** of your portfolio to plan your task.

3. When you have finished, complete the student reflection note on **page 46** of your portfolio.

ACT 3

ACT 3, PART 1

In this part of the act you will:

- Create a character **profile** of Cecily Cardew.
- See **Lady Bracknell** arrive at the Manor House to help move the play toward its conclusion.
- Explore the power struggle that takes place between Lady Bracknell and Jack.

SCENE

Morning-room at the Manor House. GWENDOLEN and CECILY are at the window, looking out into the garden.

GWENDOLEN

The fact that they did not follow us at once into the house, as any one else would have done, seems to me to show that they have some sense of shame left.

CECILY

They have been eating muffins. That looks like repentance[1].

1. guilt

GWENDOLEN

[*After a pause*] They don't seem to notice us at all. Couldn't you cough?

CECILY

But I haven't got a cough.

GWENDOLEN

They're looking at us. What effrontery[2]!

2. boldness

CECILY

They're approaching. That's very forward of them.

GWENDOLEN

Let us preserve[3] a dignified silence.

3. keep

CECILY

Certainly. It's the only thing to do now.

[Enter JACK followed by ALGERNON. They whistle some dreadful popular air[4] from a British Opera]

4. tune

GWENDOLEN

This dignified silence seems to produce an unpleasant effect.

CECILY

A most distasteful one.

GWENDOLEN

But we will not be the first to speak.

CECILY

Certainly not.

GWENDOLEN

Mr Worthing, I have something very particular to ask you. Much depends on your reply.

CECILY

Gwendolen, your common sense is invaluable[5]. Mr Moncrieff, kindly answer me the following question. Why did you pretend to be my guardian's brother?

5. extremely useful

ALGERNON

In order that I might have an opportunity of meeting you.

CECILY

[*To GWENDOLEN*] That certainly seems a satisfactory explanation, does it not?

GWENDOLEN

Yes, dear, if you can believe him.

CECILY

I don't. But that does not affect the wonderful beauty of his answer.

GWENDOLEN

True. In matters of grave importance, style, not sincerity is the vital thing. Mr Worthing, what explanation can you offer to me for pretending to have a brother? Was it in order that you might have an opportunity of coming up to town to see me as often as possible?

JACK

Can you doubt it, Miss Fairfax?

GWENDOLEN

I have the gravest doubts upon the subject. But I intend to crush them. This is not the moment for German scepticism[6]. [*Moving to CECILY*] Their explanations appear to be quite satisfactory, especially Mr Worthing's. That seems to me to have the stamp of truth upon it.

CECILY

I am more than content with what Mr Moncrieff said. His voice alone inspires one with absolute credulity[7].

GWENDOLEN

Then you think we should forgive them?

CECILY

Yes. I mean no.

GWENDOLEN

True! I had forgotten. There are principles at stake that one cannot surrender. Which of us should tell them? The task is not a pleasant one.

6. doubt

7. willingness to believe

CECILY

Could we not both speak at the same time?

GWENDOLEN

An excellent idea! I nearly always speak at the same time as other people. Will you take the time from me?

CECILY

Certainly. [*GWENDOLEN beats time with uplifted finger*]

GWENDOLEN AND CECILY

[*Speaking together*] Your Christian names are still an insuperable[8] barrier. That is all!

8. impossible to overcome

JACK AND ALGERNON

[*Speaking together*] Our Christian names! Is that all? But we are going to be christened this afternoon.

GWENDOLEN

[*To JACK*] For my sake you are prepared to do this terrible thing?

JACK

I am.

CECILY

[*To ALGERNON*] To please me you are ready to face this fearful ordeal?

ALGERNON

I am!

GWENDOLEN

How absurd to talk of the equality of the sexes! Where questions of self-sacrifice are concerned, men are infinitely beyond us.

JACK

We are. [*Clasps hands with ALGERNON*]

CECILY

They have moments of physical courage of which we women know absolutely nothing.

GWENDOLEN

[*To JACK*] Darling!

ALGERNON

[*To CECILY*] Darling! [*They fall into each other's arms*]

[*Enter MERRIMAN. When he enters he coughs loudly, seeing the situation*]

MERRIMAN

Ahem! Ahem! Lady Bracknell!

JACK

Good heavens!

[*Enter LADY BRACKNELL. The couples separate in alarm. Exit MERRIMAN*]

LADY BRACKNELL

Gwendolen! What does this mean?

GWENDOLEN

Merely that I am engaged to be married to Mr Worthing, mamma.

LADY BRACKNELL

Come here. Sit down. Sit down immediately. Hesitation of any kind is a sign of mental decay in the young, of physical weakness in the old. [*Turns to JACK*] Apprised⁹, sir, of my daughter's sudden flight by her trusty maid, whose confidence I purchased by means of a small coin, I followed her at once by a luggage train. Her unhappy father is, I am glad to say, under the impression that she is attending a more than usually lengthy lecture by the University Extension Scheme on the Influence of a permanent income on Thought. I do not propose to undeceive him. Indeed I have never undeceived him on any question. I would consider it wrong. But of course, you will clearly understand that all communication between yourself and my daughter must cease immediately from this moment. On this point, as indeed on all points, I am firm.

9. informed

JACK

I am engaged to be married to Gwendolen, Lady Bracknell!

LADY BRACKNELL

You are nothing of the kind, sir. And now, as regards Algernon! . . . Algernon!

ALGERNON

Yes, Aunt Augusta.

LADY BRACKNELL

May I ask if it is in this house that your invalid¹⁰ friend Mr Bunbury resides¹¹?

10. sick

11. lives

ALGERNON

[*Stammering*] Oh! No! Bunbury doesn't live here. Bunbury is somewhere else at present. In fact, Bunbury is dead.

LADY BRACKNELL

Dead! When did Mr Bunbury die? His death must have been extremely sudden.

ALGERNON

[*Airily*] Oh! I killed Bunbury this afternoon. I mean poor Bunbury died this afternoon.

LADY BRACKNELL

What did he die of?

ALGERNON

Bunbury? Oh, he was quite exploded.

LADY BRACKNELL

Exploded! Was he the victim of a revolutionary outrage? I was not aware that Mr Bunbury was interested in social legislation[12]. If so, he is well punished for his morbidity[13].

ALGERNON

My dear Aunt Augusta, I mean he was found out! The doctors found out that Bunbury could not live, that is what I mean—so Bunbury died.

LADY BRACKNELL

He seems to have had great confidence in the opinion of his physicians[14]. I am glad, however, that he made up his mind at the last to some definite course of action, and acted under proper medical advice. And now that we have finally got rid of this Mr Bunbury, may I ask, Mr Worthing, who is that young person whose hand my nephew Algernon is now holding in what seems to me a peculiarly[15] unnecessary manner?

JACK

That lady is Miss Cecily Cardew, my ward. [*Lady Bracknell bows coldly to CECILY*]

ALGERNON

I am engaged to be married to Cecily, Aunt Augusta.

LADY BRACKNELL

I beg your pardon?

CECILY

Mr Moncrieff and I are engaged to be married, Lady Bracknell.

12. laws that protect the weaker members of society
13. an unhealthy interest in disease and death
14. doctors
15. more than usually

LADY BRACKNELL

[*With a shiver, crossing to the sofa and sitting down*] I do not know whether there is anything peculiarly exciting in the air of this particular part of Hertfordshire, but the number of engagements that go on seems to me considerably above the proper average that statistics have laid down for our guidance. I think some preliminary[16] enquiry on my part would not be out of place. Mr Worthing, is Miss Cardew at all connected with any of the larger railway stations in London? I merely desire information. Until yesterday I had no idea that there were any families or persons whose origin was a Terminus[17]. [*Jack looks perfectly furious, but restrains himself*]

16. introductory

17. the end of a railway line

JACK

[*In a clear, cold voice*] Miss Cardew is the granddaughter of the late Mr Thomas Cardew of 149 Belgrave Square, S.W.; Gervase Park, Dorking, Surrey; and the Sporran, Fifeshire, N.B[18].

18. North Britain, i.e. Scotland

LADY BRACKNELL

That sounds not unsatisfactory. Three addresses always inspire confidence, even in tradesmen. But what proof have I of their authenticity[19]?

19. accuracy

JACK

I have carefully preserved the Court Guides of the period. They are open to your inspection, Lady Bracknell.

LADY BRACKNELL

[*Grimly*] I have known strange errors in that publication.

JACK

Miss Cardew's family solicitors are Messrs[20] Markby, Markby, and Markby.

20. formal title for more than one man

LADY BRACKNELL

Markby, Markby, and Markby? A firm of the very highest position in their profession. Indeed I am told that one of the Mr Markbys is occasionally to be seen at dinner parties. So far I am satisfied.

JACK

[*Very irritably*] How extremely kind of you, Lady Bracknell! I have also in my possession, you will be pleased to hear, certificates of Miss Cardew's birth, baptism, whooping cough, registration, vaccination, confirmation, and the measles; both the German and the English variety.

LADY BRACKNELL

Ah! A life crowded with incident, I see; though perhaps somewhat too exciting for a young girl. I am not myself in favour of premature experiences. [*Rises, looks at her watch*] Gwendolen! the time approaches for our departure. We have not a moment to lose. As a matter of form, Mr Worthing, I had better ask you if Miss Cardew has any little fortune?

JACK

Oh! about a hundred and thirty thousand pounds in the Funds[21]. That is all. Good-bye, Lady Bracknell. So pleased to have seen you.

21. government stocks, considered to be a safe investment

LADY BRACKNELL

[*Sitting down again*] A moment, Mr Worthing. A hundred and thirty thousand pounds! And in the Funds! Miss Cardew seems to me a most attractive young lady, now that I look at her. Few girls of the present day have any really solid qualities, any of the qualities that last, and improve with time. We live, I regret to say, in

an age of surfaces. [*To CECILY*] Come over here, dear. [*CECILY goes across*] Pretty child! your dress is sadly simple, and your hair seems almost as Nature might have left it. But we can soon alter all that. A thoroughly experienced French maid produces a really marvellous result in a very brief space of time. I remember recommending one to young Lady Lancing, and after three months her own husband did not know her.

JACK

And after six months nobody knew her.

LADY BRACKNELL

[*Glares at JACK for a few moments. Then bends, with a practised smile, to CECILY*] Kindly turn round, sweet child. [*CECILY turns completely round*] No, the side view is what I want. [*CECILY presents her profile*] Yes, quite as I expected. There are distinct social possibilities in your profile. The two weak points in our age are its want of principle and its want of profile. The chin a little higher, dear. Style largely depends on the way the chin is worn. They are worn very high, just at present. Algernon!

ALGERNON

Yes, Aunt Augusta!

LADY BRACKNELL

There are distinct social possibilities in Miss Cardew's profile.

ALGERNON

Cecily is the sweetest, dearest, prettiest girl in the whole world. And I don't care twopence about social possibilities.

LADY BRACKNELL

Never speak disrespectfully of Society, Algernon. Only people who can't get into it do that. [*To CECILY*] Dear child, of course you know that Algernon has nothing but his debts to depend upon. But I do not approve of mercenary[22] marriages. When I married Lord Bracknell I had no fortune of any kind. But I never dreamed for a moment of allowing that to stand in my way. Well, I suppose I must give my consent.

22. based on money

ALGERNON

Thank you, Aunt Augusta.

LADY BRACKNELL

Cecily, you may kiss me!

CECILY

[*Kisses her*] Thank you, Lady Bracknell.

LADY BRACKNELL

You may also address me as Aunt Augusta for the future.

CECILY

Thank you, Aunt Augusta.

LADY BRACKNELL

The marriage, I think, had better take place quite soon.

ALGERNON

Thank you, Aunt Augusta.

CECILY

Thank you, Aunt Augusta.

LADY BRACKNELL

To speak frankly, I am not in favour of long engagements. They give people the opportunity of finding out each other's character before marriage, which I think is never advisable.

JACK

I beg your pardon for interrupting you, Lady Bracknell, but this engagement is quite out of the question. I am Miss Cardew's guardian, and she cannot marry without my consent until she comes of age. That consent I absolutely decline to give.

LADY BRACKNELL

Upon what grounds may I ask? Algernon is an extremely, I may almost say an ostentatiously[23], eligible young man. He has nothing, but he looks everything. What more can one desire?

23. showy/extravagant

JACK

It pains me very much to have to speak frankly to you, Lady Bracknell, about your nephew, but the fact is that I do not approve at all of his moral character. I suspect him of being untruthful.

[*ALGERNON and CECILY look at him in indignant[24] amazement*]

24. annoyed

LADY BRACKNELL

Untruthful! My nephew Algernon? Impossible! He is an Oxonian[25].

25. A past student of the University of Oxford, one of England's most respected universities. Oscar Wilde also attended the university.

JACK

I fear there can be no possible doubt about the matter. This afternoon during my temporary absence in London on an important question of romance, he obtained admission[26] to my house by means of the false pretence[27] of being my brother. Under an assumed name he drank, I've just been informed by my butler, an entire pint bottle of my Perrier-Jouet, Brut, '89[28]; a wine I was specially reserving for myself. Continuing his disgraceful deception[29], he succeeded in the course of the afternoon in alienating the affections of my only ward. He subsequently[30] stayed to tea, and devoured[31] every single muffin. And what makes his conduct all the more heartless is, that he was perfectly well aware from the first that I have no brother, that I never had a brother, and that I don't intend to have a brother, not even of any kind. I distinctly told him so myself yesterday afternoon.

26. entry

27. pretending

28. A dry champagne. It was a favourite drink of Oscar Wilde's.

29. lies/trickery

30. later

31. quickly ate

LADY BRACKNELL

Ahem! Mr Worthing, after careful consideration I have decided entirely to overlook my nephew's conduct to you.

JACK

That is very generous of you, Lady Bracknell. My own decision, however, is unalterable[32]. I decline to give my consent.

LADY BRACKNELL

[*To CECILY*] Come here, sweet child. [*CECILY goes over*] How old are you, dear?

CECILY

Well, I am really only eighteen, but I always admit to twenty when I go to evening parties.

LADY BRACKNELL

You are perfectly right in making some slight alteration. Indeed, no woman should ever be quite accurate about her age. It looks so calculating . . . [*In a meditative manner*] Eighteen, but admitting to twenty at evening parties. Well, it will not be very long before you are of age and free from the restraints of tutelage[33]. So I don't think your guardian's consent is, after all, a matter of any importance.

JACK

Pray excuse me, Lady Bracknell, for interrupting you again, but it is only fair to tell you that according to the terms of her grandfather's will Miss Cardew does not come legally of age till she is thirty-five.

LADY BRACKNELL

That does not seem to me to be a grave[34] objection. Thirty-five is a very attractive age. London society is full of women of the very highest birth who have, of their own free choice, remained thirty-five for years. Lady Dumbleton is an instance in point. To my own knowledge she has been thirty-five ever since she arrived at the age of forty, which was many years ago now. I see no reason why our dear Cecily should not be even still more attractive at the age you mention than she is at present. There will be a large accumulation[35] of property.

CECILY

Algy, could you wait for me till I was thirty-five?

32. not able to be changed

33. the protection of a guardian

34. serious

35. gaining

ALGERNON

Of course I could, Cecily. You know I could.

CECILY

Yes, I felt it instinctively[36], but I couldn't wait all that time. I hate waiting even five minutes for anybody. It always makes me rather cross. I am not punctual[37] myself, I know, but I do like punctuality in others, and waiting, even to be married, is quite out of the question.

ALGERNON

Then what is to be done, Cecily?

CECILY

I don't know, Mr Moncrieff.

LADY BRACKNELL

My dear Mr Worthing, as Miss Cardew states positively that she cannot wait till she is thirty-five—a remark which I am bound[38] to say seems to me to show a somewhat impatient nature—I would beg of you to reconsider your decision.

JACK

But my dear Lady Bracknell, the matter is entirely in your own hands. The moment you consent to my marriage with Gwendolen, I will most gladly allow your nephew to form an alliance[39] with my ward.

36. without thought

37. on time

38. required/obliged

39. relationship

LADY BRACKNELL

[*Rising and drawing herself up*] You must be quite aware that what you propose is out of the question.

JACK

Then a passionate celibacy[40] is all that any of us can look forward to.

LADY BRACKNELL

That is not the destiny I propose for Gwendolen. Algernon, of course, can choose for himself. [*Pulls out her watch*] Come, dear [*GWENDOLEN rises*], we have already missed five, if not six, trains. To miss any more might expose us to comment on the platform.

[*Enter Dr CHASUBLE*]

CHASUBLE

Everything is quite ready for the christenings.

LADY BRACKNELL

The christenings, sir! Is not that somewhat premature[41]?

CHASUBLE

[*Looking rather puzzled, and pointing to JACK and ALGERNON*] Both these gentlemen have expressed a desire for immediate baptism.

LADY BRACKNELL

At their age? The idea is grotesque[42] and irreligious[43]! Algernon, I forbid you to be baptised. I will not hear of such excesses[44]. Lord Bracknell would be highly displeased if he learned that that was the way in which you wasted your time and money.

CHASUBLE

Am I to understand then that there are to be no christenings at all this afternoon?

JACK

I don't think that, as things are now, it would be of much practical value to either of us, Dr Chasuble.

CHASUBLE

I am grieved to hear such sentiments from you, Mr Worthing. They

40. unmarried life

41. too early

42. ridiculous
43. unholy
44. indulgence/waste

savour of the heretical[45] views of the Anabaptists[46], views that I have completely refuted[47] in four of my unpublished sermons. However, as your present mood seems to be one peculiarly secular[48], I will return to the church at once. Indeed, I have just been informed by the pew-opener that for the last hour and a half Miss Prism has been waiting for me in the vestry[49].

LADY BRACKNELL

[*Starting*] Miss Prism! Did I hear you mention a Miss Prism?

CHASUBLE

Yes, Lady Bracknell. I am on my way to join her.

LADY BRACKNELL

Pray allow me to detain[50] you for a moment. This matter may prove to be one of vital importance to Lord Bracknell and myself. Is this Miss Prism a female of repellent[51] aspect[52], remotely[53] connected with education?

CHASUBLE

[*Somewhat indignantly*[54]] She is the most cultivated[55] of ladies, and the very picture of respectability.

LADY BRACKNELL

It is obviously the same person. May I ask what position she holds in your household?

CHASUBLE

[*Severely*] I am a celibate[56], madam.

JACK

[*Interposing*[57]] Miss Prism, Lady Bracknell, has been for the last three years Miss Cardew's esteemed[58] governess and valued companion.

LADY BRACKNELL

In spite of what I hear of her, I must see her at once. Let her be sent for.

CHASUBLE

[*Looking off*] She approaches; she is nigh[59].

45. beliefs that go against the accepted teachings of the church
46. A sixteenth-century religious group that believed in baptism for adults only.
47. proved wrong
48. non-religious

49. The room in a church where the vicar or priest's clothing is kept.

50. delay

51. off-putting
52. features
53. loosely/hardly

54. angrily
55. well-educated

56. unmarried person

57. interrupting

58. respected

59. near

ACTION SUMMARY ACT 3, PART 1

- Gwendolen and Cecily are looking out the window at Jack and Algernon. Gwendolen is annoyed that the men have have not followed them inside.

- When the men do come inside, Cecily asks Algernon why he lied about his name. He explains that he only did it so he could spend time with her.

- Gwendolen asks Jack if he lied about his name so he could come to town and spend time with her. Jack says that this is true.

- Gwendolen and Cecily agree to forgive Jack and Algernon for lying. However, they inform them that their names are still a barrier to marriage.

- Jack and Algernon tell the women that they are both due to be christened Ernest that evening. Gwendolen and Cecily are delighted to hear this news.

- Merriman interrupts the embracing couples and tells them that Lady Bracknell has arrived.

- Gwendolen and Jack tell Lady Bracknell that they are engaged. Lady Bracknell tells them that they are not.

- Lady Bracknell asks Algernon if he is at the Manor House to visit Mr Bunbury. Algernon tells Lady Bracknell that Bunbury does not live in the house and that he is, in fact, dead.

- When Lady Bracknell sees Cecily holding hands with Algernon, Cecily informs Lady Bracknell that she is engaged to Algernon.

- Lady Bracknell questions Jack about Cecily's family background and is pleased to hear that she is a wealthy young woman with a clear family history.

- Lady Bracknell gives her consent for Algernon and Cecily to marry.

- Jack objects to the match because he knows Algernon to be an untruthful person.

- Jack also informs Lady Bracknell that as he is Cecily's guardian she needs his permission to marry until she comes of age. According to her grandfather's will, Cecily can not choose to marry for herself until she is thirty-five. She is only eighteen.

- Jack explains that he will only give his consent for Cecily to marry Algernon if Lady Bracknell gives her permission for him and Gwendolen to wed. Lady Bracknell is furious and rises to leave.

- Before Lady Bracknell can leave, Dr Chasuble enters to see if the men are ready for their christenings. Jack tells him that there no longer seems to be any point in carrying out the baptisms.

- Lady Bracknell recognises Dr Chasuble's description of Miss Prism and asks for her to be sent for at once.

A. REVIEWING

1. Do you believe that Gwendolen and Cecily are truly angry at Jack and Algernon at the start of Act 3?

2. Based on what she says about marriage, do you think Lady Bracknell is a romantic person?

3. How do the other characters treat Dr Chasuble at the end of this part of Act 3?

4. Rank the three most humorous lines in this part of Act 3, briefly explaining why you found each line humorous.

B. EXPLORING

Power Struggle

As Lady Bracknell will not allow Jack to marry Gwendolen, Jack will not give his permission for Cecily to marry Algernon. Lady Bracknell and Jack struggle for power and control over the situation.

Use the power grid on **page 48** of your portfolio to trace which character is in control at key points in the dialogue. When the discussion comes to a close, write the name of the character you think finished in control into the Central Control Unit, along with the reason why.

• Begin at Lady Bracknell's line 'To speak frankly, I am not in favour of long engagements' at the top of **page 119**.

• End at Lady Bracknell's line 'To miss any more might expose us to comment on the platform' on **page 122**.

C. ORAL LANGUAGE

1. Speaking Together

Pair Activity

In this part of the play, Jack and Algernon and Gwendolen and Cecily speak together to make their points (see **page 111**).

a. In pairs, discuss what you think of all four characters. Then turn to **page 50** of your portfolio and write a sentence that you agree on to describe each character.

b. When you are finished, you must read out your sentences to the class at the same time, just like the pairs in the play. Try to keep in time!

2. Debating Gender in Victorian England

Group Activity

> **GWENDOLEN:** How absurd to talk of the equality of the sexes! Where questions of self-sacrifice are concerned, men are infinitely beyond us.

Using Gwendolen's quote as a starting point, research and debate the equality of the sexes in Victorian England.

• One team should support the view that Victorian men were expected to sacrifice more than Victorian women were expected to sacrifice.

• The other team should support the view that Victorian society required women to give up more than men.

D. CREATING

Cecily Cardew's Profile

In Act 3 Lady Bracknell says, 'There are distinct social possibilities in Miss Cardew's profile.'

The word 'profile' has three meanings here:

1. The outline of Cecily's face.

2. Cecily's character.

3. Cecily's place in society.

With these meanings in mind, go to **page 51** of your portfolio and write into the silhouette the qualities Cecily Cardew has that would make her a suitable wife in the eyes of Lady Bracknell.

ACT 3, PART 2

In this part of the act you will:

- Witness the **resolution** of the conflict between the two main couples.
- Discover the **truth** about Jack's family background.
- Explore Oscar Wilde's use of **suspense** and **epigrams** to entertain his audience.

[*Enter MISS PRISM hurriedly*]

MISS PRISM

I was told you expected me in the vestry, dear Canon. I have been waiting for you there for an hour and three quarters. [*Catches sight of Lady Bracknell who has fixed her with a stony glare. MISS PRISM grows pale and quails[1]. She looks anxiously round as if desirous[2] to escape*]

1. shows fear
2. wanting

LADY BRACKNELL

[*In a severe, judicial[3] voice*] Prism! [*MISS PRISM bows her head in shame*] Come here, Prism! [*MISS PRISM approaches in a humble manner*] Prism! Where is that baby? [*General consternation[4]. The Canon starts back in horror. ALGERNON and JACK pretend to be anxious to shield CECILY and GWENDOLEN from hearing the details of a terrible public scandal*] Twenty-eight years ago, Prism, you left Lord Bracknell's house, Number 104, Upper Grosvenor Square, in charge of a perambulator[5] that contained a baby, of the male sex. You never returned. A few weeks later, through the elaborate investigations of the Metropolitan police, the perambulator was discovered at midnight, standing by itself in a remote corner of Bayswater. It contained the manuscript of a three-volume novel of more than usually revolting sentimentality. [*MISS PRISM starts in involuntary indignation[6]*] But the baby was not there! [*Everyone looks at MISS PRISM*] Prism! Where is that baby? [*A pause*]

3. judge-like

4. anxiety/panic

5. pram

6. anger

MISS PRISM

Lady Bracknell, I admit with shame that I do not know. I only wish I did. The plain facts of the case are these. On the morning of the day you mention, a day that is for ever branded on my memory,

7. spacious/roomy

8. absent-mindedness
9. put
10. pram

I prepared as usual to take the baby out in its perambulator. I had also with me a somewhat old, but capacious[7] hand-bag in which I had intended to place the manuscript of a work of fiction that I had written during my few unoccupied hours. In a moment of mental abstraction[8], for which I never can forgive myself, I deposited[9] the manuscript in the basinette[10], and placed the baby in the hand-bag.

JACK

[*Who had been listening attentively*] But where did you deposit the hand-bag?

MISS PRISM

Do not ask me, Mr Worthing.

JACK

Miss Prism, this is a matter of no small importance to me. I insist on knowing where you deposited the hand-bag that contained that infant.

MISS PRISM

I left it in the cloak-room of one of the larger railway stations in London.

JACK

What railway station?

MISS PRISM

[*Quite crushed*] Victoria. The Brighton line. [*Sinks into a chair*]

JACK

I must retire to my room for a moment. Gwendolen, wait here for me.

GWENDOLEN

If you are not too long, I will wait here for you all my life.

[*Exit JACK in great excitement*]

CHASUBLE

What do you think this means, Lady Bracknell?

LADY BRACKNELL

I dare not even suspect, Dr Chasuble. I need hardly tell you that in families of high position strange coincidences are not supposed to occur. They are hardly considered the thing.

[*Noises heard overhead as if some one was throwing trunks about. Everyone looks up*]

CECILY

Uncle Jack seems strangely agitated[11].

11. troubled

CHASUBLE

Your guardian has a very emotional nature.

LADY BRACKNELL

This noise is extremely unpleasant. It sounds as if he was having an argument. I dislike arguments of any kind. They are always vulgar[12], and often convincing.

12. tasteless

CHASUBLE

[*Looking up*] It has stopped now. [*The noise is redoubled[13]*]

13. more intense

LADY BRACKNELL

I wish he would arrive at some conclusion.

GWENDOLEN

This suspense is terrible. I hope it will last. [*Enter JACK with a hand-bag of black leather in his hand*]

JACK

[*Rushing over to MISS PRISM*] Is this the hand-bag, Miss Prism? Examine it carefully before you speak. The happiness of more than one life depends on your answer.

MISS PRISM

[*Calmly*] It seems to be mine. Yes, here is the injury it received through the upsetting of a Gower Street omnibus[14] in younger and happier days. Here is the stain on the lining caused by the explosion of a temperance beverage[15], an incident that occurred at Leamington. And here, on the lock, are my initials. I had forgotten that in an extravagant mood I had had them placed there. The bag is undoubtedly mine. I am delighted to have it so unexpectedly restored[16] to me. It has been a great inconvenience being without it all these years.

14. bus

15. non-alcoholic drink

16. returned

JACK

[*In a pathetic voice*] Miss Prism, more is restored to you than this hand-bag. I was the baby you placed in it.

MISS PRISM

[*Amazed*] You?

JACK

[*Embracing her*] Yes—mother!

MISS PRISM

[*Recoiling*[17] *in indignant astonishment*] Mr Worthing! I am unmarried!

17. drawing back

JACK

Unmarried! I do not deny that is a serious blow. But after all, who has the right to cast a stone[18] against one who has suffered? Cannot repentance[19] wipe out an act of folly[20]? Why should there be one law for men, and another for women? Mother, I forgive you. [*Tries to embrace her again*]

18. A Biblical reference to John 8:7. Stoning was the biblical punishment for adultery. When a woman accused of adultery was brought before Jesus he said, 'Let the one who has never sinned throw the first stone!'
19. remorse/being sorry
20. foolishness

MISS PRISM

[*Still more indignant*] Mr Worthing, there is some error. [*Pointing to LADY BRACKNELL*] There is the lady who can tell you who you really are.

JACK

[*After a pause*] Lady Bracknell, I hate to seem inquisitive[21], but would you kindly inform me who I am?

21. nosy

22. as a result

LADY BRACKNELL

I am afraid that the news I have to give you will not altogether please you. You are the son of my poor sister, Mrs Moncrieff, and consequently[22] Algernon's elder brother.

JACK

 Algy's elder brother! Then I have a brother after all. I knew I had a brother! I always said I had a brother! Cecily,—how could you have ever doubted that I had a brother? [*Seizes hold of ALGERNON*] Dr Chasuble, my unfortunate brother. Miss Prism, my unfortunate brother. Gwendolen, my unfortunate brother. Algy, you young scoundrel, you will have to treat me with more respect in the future. You have never behaved to me like a brother in all your life.

ALGERNON

Well, not till today, old boy, I admit. I did my best, however, though I was out of practice.

[*Shakes hands*]

23. first name, especially one given at baptism

GWENDOLEN

[*To JACK*] My own! But what own are you? What is your Christian name[23], now that you have become someone else?

JACK

24. final

Good heavens!—I had quite forgotten that point. Your decision on the subject of my name is irrevocable[24], I suppose?

GWENDOLEN

I never change, except in my affections.

25. good/high-class

CECILY

What a noble[25] nature you have, Gwendolen!

JACK

Then the question had better be cleared up at once. Aunt Augusta, a moment. At the time when Miss Prism left me in the hand-bag, had I been christened already?

LADY BRACKNELL

Every luxury that money could buy, including christening, had been lavished on you by your fond and doting parents.

JACK

Then I was christened! That is settled. Now, what name was I given? Let me know the worst.

LADY BRACKNELL

Being the eldest son you were naturally christened after your father.

JACK

[*Irritably*] Yes, but what was my father's Christian name?

LADY BRACKNELL

[*Meditatively*[26]] I cannot at the present moment recall what the General's Christian name was. But I have no doubt he had one. He was eccentric[27], I admit. But only in later years. And that was the result of the Indian climate, and marriage, and indigestion, and other things of that kind.

JACK

Algy! Can't you recollect[28] what our father's Christian name was?

ALGERNON

My dear boy, we were never even on speaking terms. He died before I was a year old.

JACK

His name would appear in the Army Lists[29] of the period, I suppose, Aunt Augusta?

LADY BRACKNELL

The General was essentially a man of peace, except in his domestic[30] life. But I have no doubt his name would appear in any military directory.

JACK

The Army Lists of the last forty years are here. These delightful records should have been my constant study. [*Rushes to bookcase and tears the books out*] M. Generals . . . Mallam, Maxbohm, Magley—what ghastly[31] names they have—Markby, Migsby, Mobbs, Moncrieff! Lieutenant 1840, Captain, Lieutenant-Colonel, Colonel, General 1869, Christian names, Ernest John. [*Puts book very quietly down and speaks quite calmly*] I always told you, Gwendolen, my name was Ernest, didn't I? Well, it is Ernest after all. I mean it naturally is Ernest.

LADY BRACKNELL

Yes, I remember now that the General was called Ernest. I knew I had some particular reason for disliking the name.

26. thoughtfully

27. strange

28. remember

29. A list of names of those serving in the British Army.

30. home

31. awful

GWENDOLEN

Ernest! My own Ernest! I felt from the first that you could have no other name!

JACK

Gwendolen, it is a terrible thing for a man to find out suddenly that all his life he has been speaking nothing but the truth. Can you forgive me?

GWENDOLEN

I can. For I feel that you are sure to change.

JACK

My own one!

CHASUBLE

[*To MISS PRISM*] Laetitia! [*Embraces her*]

MISS PRISM

[*Enthusiastically*] Frederick! At last!

ALGERNON

Cecily! [*Embraces her*] At last!

JACK

Gwendolen! [*Embraces her*] At last!

32. unimportance/foolishness

LADY BRACKNELL

My nephew, you seem to be displaying signs of triviality[32].

JACK

On the contrary, Aunt Augusta, I've now realised for the first time in my life the vital Importance of Being Earnest.

TABLEAU

CURTAIN

ACTION SUMMARY ACT 3, PART 2

- Miss Prism enters the room and seems anxious when she sees Lady Bracknell. Lady Bracknell recognises Miss Prism and demands to know what happened to a baby that went missing while in Miss Prism's care.

- We discover that twenty-eight years ago, Miss Prism accidentally lost a baby boy by placing the novel she was writing in the baby's pram and putting the baby in her handbag.

- Jack immediately takes interest in Miss Prism's story and asks her where she left the handbag. Miss Prism tells him it was at a train station.

- Jack leaves the room and goes upstairs. As the other characters wait for his return, loud noises can be heard.

- When Jack returns with a handbag, Miss Prism confirms that it is the same one she lost. She is happy to have it returned.

- Jack calls Miss Prism 'mother', believing her to be one of the parents he never knew. Miss Prism tells Jack she is not his mother, but Lady Bracknell can tell him the identity of his mother.

- Lady Bracknell explains that Jack is the son of her sister, Mrs Moncrieff. This means that Jack is Algernon's older brother.

- Gwendolen still insists on knowing Jack's real Christian (first) name.

- Lady Bracknell tells Jack that he was named after his father, an Army General. However, she cannot remember General Moncrieff's first name. Algernon does not know his father's Christian name either, as the General died when he was a baby.

- Jack remembers that he has a book of Army records, which he rushes to check. When he inspects the book he finds out that his father was called Ernest John.

- Gwendolen is delighted to hear that Jack's real name is Ernest.

- Dr Chasuble embraces Miss Prism, Algernon embraces Cecily and Jack embraces Gwendolen.

- The plays ends with Jack proclaiming to Lady Bracknell, 'I've now realised for the first time in my life the vital Importance of Being Earnest.'

A. REVIEWING

1. What does Miss Prism put into the pram instead of the baby?

2. Who are Jack's parents?

3. Do you agree with Jack when he says to Algernon, 'You have never behaved to me like a brother in all your life'?

4. How does Oscar Wilde build suspense at the end of Act 3?

5. What do you think Jack means in the final line of the play?

B. EXPLORING

Oscar Worthy

1. In class or at home, watch a film adaptation of *The Importance of Being Earnest*. There have been two versions of the play made for the big screen:

   • 1952; directed by Anthony Asquith; starring Michael Redgrave (Jack), Michael Denison (Algernon), Edith Evans (Lady Bracknell), Dorothy Tutin (Cecily), Joan Greenwood (Gwendolen), Margaret Rutherford (Miss Prism) and Miles Malleson (Canon Chasuble)

   • 1992; directed by Oliver Parker; starring Colin Firth (Jack), Rupert Everett (Algy), Judi Dench (Lady Bracknell), Reese Witherspoon (Cecily), Frances O'Connor (Gwendolen), Anna Massey (Miss Prism) and Tom Wilkinson (Canon Chasuble)

2. Turn to **page 52** of your portfolio to write a film review of the version you have watched. As well as explaining what you liked or did not like about the film, you should comment on any differences between the film and the play.

C. ORAL LANGUAGE

Building Suspense

Group Activity

Towards the end of Act 3 Gwendolen remarks, 'This suspense is terrible. I hope it will last.' In other words, despite saying it is 'terrible', Gwendolen is enjoying the uncertainty of the moment.

Suspense is often used in drama to keep audiences on the edge of their seats and to keep them watching.

1. In groups, brainstorm moments of suspense you have seen in drama, film or on TV. For example, a cliffhanger at the end of an episode of *EastEnders* or not knowing if a character in a film will live or die.

2. In your groups, write a short scene about a moment of great suspense.

3. Perform your scene for the class.

D. CREATING

1. Create Your Own Epigram

An epigram is a short statement that is easily quoted. It is usually clever or witty.

Oscar Wilde was the master of the epigram and his words are often quoted. Turn to **page 54** of your portfolio to read some of Wilde's famous oneliners and to make up one of your own!

2. Modern-day General Moncrieff

Near the end of Act 3 we find out that General Moncrieff, Algernon and Jack's father, was stationed in India as part of his military service. One of his duties would have been sending regular formal letters to his commanders in Britain.

Imagine you are an Irish general working abroad on a peace-keeping mission. Turn to **page 55** of your portfolio to write a formal email to your commanders at home.

3. Tableau

Group Activity

The Importance of Being Earnest ends with a tableau. A tableau is a pause during or at the end of a play when all the actors freeze silently in their position on stage.

In groups of seven:

- Choose a character each (Lady Bracknell, Gwendolen, Jack, Miss Prism, Dr Chasuble, Algernon, Cecily).
- Perform the tableau at the end of the play. Pay attention to any final directions that apply to your character (given in square brackets in the play). Try to show what your character is feeling in your facial expressions and the way you position your body.

E. REFLECTING

1. Character File

Turn to the Character File section of your portfolio and record your impressions of **Algernon**, **Jack**, **Gwendolen**, **Cecily**, **Lady Bracknell**, **Miss Prism** and **Dr Chasuble** based on Act 3.

2. Mapping the Plot

Pair Activity

With your partner, turn to **page 5** of your portfolio and write a six sentences to sum up the main action in Act 3.

3. Act 3 Word Search

Go to **page 67** of your portfolio to complete the Act 3 word search.

OVERVIEW OF ACT 3

The couples reconcile

- At the beginning of Act 3, it is clear that Gwendolen and Cecily are not really angry at Jack and Algernon. They want to forgive them, but they must play along with the **social rules** that require the men to win the women's affections. As Gwendolen says:

> *In matters of grave importance, style, not sincerity is the vital thing.*

Again, Wilde is **mocking Victorian society** for being more interested in **keeping up appearances** than in the reality of a situation.

- Even when both women forgive their partners, Wilde keeps up the **conflict** between them. Cecily and Gwendolen still have a problem with the men's Christian names. The two women voice their concern by speaking together:

> *Your Christian names are still an insuperable barrier. That is all!*

The characters speaking at the same time provides **comedy**. However, Wilde is also suggesting that members of the upper class do not speak based on personal feeling, but according to the **conventions and customs of society**. As a result, they are all the same.

- Algernon and Jack are both willing to change their first names to please the women. Wilde uses **hyperbole** (exaggeration) to make the point that the men's sacrifice is actually quite small and meaningless. Gwendolen and Cecily refer to their offer to be baptised as a 'terrible thing' and a 'fearful ordeal'.

- Wilde also uses hyperbole and **satire** to comment on the difference between the genders in Victorian society, in which women had fewer choices and had to make more personal sacrifices than men. Gwendolen says:

> *How absurd to talk of the equality of the sexes! Where questions of self-sacrifice are concerned, men are infinitely beyond us.*

Lady Bracknell arrives

- Lady Bracknell's arrival interrupts the **romantic comedy** that has been unfolding in Act 3. Her presence provides a cold reminder of the importance of social rules in all matters, especially **marriage**. Lady Bracknell reminds Gwendolen that she cannot be engaged to Jack without her permission.

- Lady Bracknell is pleased when Algernon tells her that his fake friend Bunbury is dead. However, she is concerned that Bunbury might have been 'the victim of a revolutionary outrage'. This reaction highlights the **upper class fear of social change**. The aristocracy enjoy the status quo (the way things are in society) because they are the ones who benefit from it the most.

Lady Bracknell and Jack struggle for power

- Just as Lady Bracknell questioned Jack in Act 1 about his eligibility, she assesses Cecily's suitability for marriage in purely financial terms:

> *A hundred and thirty thousand pounds! And in the Funds! Miss Cardew seems to me a most attractive young lady, now that I look at her … We live, I regret to say, in an age of surfaces.*

Again, Wilde is **mocking the upper classes** for the importance they place on **wealth and appearance above character**.

- This time, Jack has the upper hand over Lady Bracknell. Cecily is Jack's ward and she must get his permission to marry Algernon. It could appear that Jack is putting his own happiness above that of Cecily and Algernon. However, it is more likely that he is using his authority to play, and beat, Lady Bracknell at her own game:

> *The moment you consent to my marriage with Gwendolen, I will most gladly allow your nephew to form an alliance with my ward.*

Miss Prism reveals Jack's past

- The end of Act 3 relies on two examples of **farce** to conclude the play. First, Miss Prism explains how she confused Jack with a book when he was a baby – a **criticism** of the willingness of the upper classes to leave their children to be raised by careless people:

> *In a moment of mental abstraction, for which I never can forgive myself, I deposited the manuscript in the basinette, and placed the baby in the hand-bag.*

Then, after Jack confirms that he was the child in the bag, neither Lady Bracknell nor Algernon can remember the name of Jack and Algernon's father, whom he was named after. This suggests that names are only of great importance to the upper classes when it suits them – usually when they have something to gain by knowing them.

Although both situations are unbelieveable, they are intended to be enjoyed for their comedy.

- Algernon and Lady Bracknell's **absurd** (illogical) forgetfulness does force Jack to search military records for his father's name and conclude the play. When Jack finds out that his father's name was Ernest John, the conflicts created by Wilde are resolved. Not only is Jack confirmed to be a true member of the upper class, he was also christened with the very name that Gwendolen insists on him having if they are to marry.

Although he thought he was lying, Jack has been telling the truth all along:

> *... it is a terrible thing for a man to find out suddenly that all his life he has been speaking nothing but the truth.*

- The play concludes with Jack telling Lady Bracknell:

> *I've now realised for the first time in my life the vital Importance of Being Earnest.*

This closing line, containing the play's title, is clever and **ambiguous** (open to debate). Once again, it draws upon the **pun** on the words 'Ernest' and 'earnest', which sound exactly the same. When Jack says he has realised the 'Importance of being Earnest', he sounds like he is accepting the importance of having the right name in snobbish society (which would please Lady Bracknell and Gwendolen). However, as it is spelled 'earnest' in the script, Jack is really recognising the importance of being a sincere person.

- Yet the final line of the play could also make us question Jack's character further. Since he arrived at this realisation by **telling lies and playing games**, we are left to wonder if Jack is a truly reformed character or if he has realised that simply appearing to be earnest can lead to personal gain. In other words, this closing line could be read as Wilde's final attack on the shallowness of Victorian high society.

ACT 3 PROJECTS

Now that you have finished Act 3, you should reflect on what you have learned by doing *one* of the projects from options A and B below.

These projects will help you to prepare for the two Classroom Based Assessments (CBAs) you will complete as part of your Junior Cycle course.

Your first CBA will be an Oral Communication Task at the end of Second Year. Your second CBA will be a Collection of Texts Task in the middle of Third Year, which will involve selecting some of your written pieces.

A. Written Task

Choose one of the following titles to write about:

- *The Importance of Being Earnest* should be renamed *The Importance of Social Class*
- This play proves that lies can be useful
- In Victorian society, love was not enough for marriage
- Satire is a powerful weapon
- Cecily Cardew is the most intelligent character in the play
- You may also make up your own question, agreed with your teacher.

Your written piece should take one of the following forms (genres):

- Essay
- Newspaper article
- Speech
- Book introduction
- Another form of your choice, agreed with your teacher.

Go to **page 57** of the portfolio to plan and write your written piece.

When you have finished, complete the student reflection note on **page 62** of your portfolio.

B. Oral Communication Task
Group Activity

In groups of three, you will create a short series of podcasts. Each episode will have a host, a co-host and an expert guest.

Episode 1: The host will open a discussion about which *theme* is the most important in the play.

Episode 2: The host will open a discussion about which *character* is the most important in the play.

Episode 3: The host will open a discussion about which *literary device* is the most important in the play.

- Each episode should last approximately three minutes and can be recorded or performed in class.
- In each episode, each member of the group will take a different role.

Turn to **page 63** of your portfolio for a description of each role and for information about how to perform and record your podcasts. You can plan this task on **page 64** of the portfolio.

When you have finished, complete the student reflection note on **page 66** of your portfolio.

EXAMINING the PLAY

- **Characters in Focus**
- **Themes in Focus**
- **Approaching Exam Questions**

Important Vocabulary

Characterisation   How a character is created. The description of how a character looks can shape our view of them. So can their actions, words and relationships with other characters. All of these things should be considered when you are forming your view of a character.

Plot   The main events in a literary work. How the story unfolds.

Theme   A repeated idea, topic or message in a literary work. In *The Importance of Being Earnest*, the main themes are identity, love and marriage, social class, and secrets and lies.

Characters in Focus

Jack Worthing

Jack appears to be a **respectable** and **serious** character. From his **humble beginnings**, found as a baby in the cloakroom of a train station, he has become a **responsible** and **dutiful** young man who takes good care of his inherited estate and his young ward, Cecily. In this way, Jack is contrasted with the reckless Algernon.

> *My dear Algy, I don't know whether you will be able to understand my real motives. You are hardly serious enough. When one is placed in the position of guardian, one has to adopt a very high moral tone on all subjects. It's one's duty to do so.*

However, it soon becomes clear that Jack and Algernon are not that different. Both men live a **double life**. When Jack leaves his country estate to visit town, he pretends to be his fictional younger brother, Ernest Worthing. It is under this name that he has been courting Gwendolen.

> *I have always pretended to have a younger brother of the name of Ernest, who lives in the Albany, and gets into the most dreadful scrapes.*

Yet Jack does not think of his own lies as being like Algernon's Bunburying. Algernon is dishonest for amusement, but Jack considers his lies to be a **necessary evil**. Jack understands that a man must always appear to be **earnest** (serious and sincere) to prosper in Victorian upper-class society.

Jack's **confident** nature is seen in Act 3, during his argument with Lady Bracknell. Despite Lady Bracknell's social position and overbearing character, Jack refuses to allow Cecily to marry Algernon until Lady Bracknell gives him permission to marry Gwendolen.

> *The moment you consent to my marriage with Gwendolen, I will most gladly allow your nephew to form an alliance with my ward.*

In the end, it turns out that Jack has been **telling the truth** about himself all along. He gets the **highly-regarded** place in society he has always wanted. Yet, how he got there proves that the most respected people are not always the most honest, but the ones who know how to play the game.

> *I've now realised for the first time in my life the vital Importance of Being Earnest.*

Algernon Moncrieff

Algernon is what the Victorians called a **dandy**. Dandies were men who wore **fashionable** clothes, used **witty** language, were **self-centered** and enjoyed a **carefree** life of **leisure** and **frivolity** (fun).

> *If I am occasionally a little over-dressed, I make up for it by being always immensely over-educated.*

When we are first introduced to Algernon in Act 1 he is playing the piano in a **luxurious** apartment. Although he knows that he cannot play 'accurately', he says that he plays with 'wonderful expression'. Putting **appearance** and **pleasure** above correctness is central to Algernon's character. Lady Bracknell says of her nephew:

> *He has nothing, but he looks everything.*

Algernon thinks nothing of ripping up his bills. He is a born **rule breaker** who favours **style over substance**.

During Act 1, Algernon eats all the cucumber sandwiches meant for his aunt, Lady Bracknell, showing his **greedy** nature. When Lady Bracknell arrives, Algernon pretends that the sandwiches never existed. This is our first clue that Algernon is **comfortable telling lies**.

Although he is often **devious**, Algernon's lies are too **clever** and **entertaining** to make the audience truly dislike him.

Algernon has invented a sick friend called Bunbury, whom he pretends to visit whenever he wants to escape a boring social engagement. This elaborate creation tells us that Algernon **dislikes duty** and that he prefers to live on **his own terms**.

> *Bunbury is perfectly invaluable.*

Algernon's Bunburying continues when he pretends to be Jack's younger brother, Ernest, in order to meet and **charm** Cecily in Act 2. Algernon seems to take nothing seriously and is **unfazed** even when his lies are uncovered. As a result, Jack accuses him of being 'perfectly **heartless**'.

However, it would seem that Algernon genuinely falls in love with Cecily, perhaps because she is as **eccentric** as he is. Algernon's feelings hint at the depths beneath his **cool exterior**.

> *I'm in love with Cecily, and that is everything.*

Gwendolen Fairfax

Gwendolen is a **sophisticated** but **shallow** character. She is a clear product of the upper-class society in which her mother, Lady Bracknell, has raised her.

> *… mamma, whose views on education are remarkably strict, has brought me up to be extremely short-sighted; it is part of her system …*

Gwendolen is **impulsive** and does not take time to get to know people. When she meets Cecily in Act 2, she makes a **snap judgment** about her:

> *I like you already more than I can say. My first impressions of people are never wrong.*

Of course, Gwendolen's impressions of Jack, the man she is planning to marry, are completely wrong. She is not as **shrewd** (clever) as she believes herself to be.

When Gwendolen mistakes Cecily as a rival for Ernest's affections, she becomes **envious** and **spiteful**.

> *If the poor fellow has been entrapped into any foolish promise I shall consider it my duty to rescue him at once, and with a firm hand.*

Gwendolen's **self-assured** attitude causes one of the central conflicts of the play when she refuses to marry a man by any other name than Ernest.

> *We live … in an age of ideals … and my ideal has always been to love someone of the name of Ernest.*

Gwendolen **knows exactly what she wants** and she will not give up until she gets it. She insists on the importance of the name Ernest until the end of the play.

> *I never change, except in my affections.*

Although Gwendolen's words and actions can be **harsh**, it is difficult to dislike her. Indeed, her **stubborn** behaviour is considered acceptable, **smart** even, in a society that viewed marrying the right man as the most important thing for young women. Furthermore, Gwendolen seems to have true feelings for Jack.

Cecily Cardew

Cecily is an **inventive** and **romantic** young woman. Like Gwendolen, she is the product of a society that has taught women to value marriage above all things.

Living a sheltered life in the country, Cecily must rely on her **imagination** to satisfy her **longing** for love and excitement. To this end, she keeps a diary where she 'usually chronicles the things that have never happened, and couldn't possibly have happened'.

Cecily fancies herself in love with Jack's younger, roguish brother without ever having met him. She goes as far as proposing to herself on his behalf, which surprises Algernon when he shows up pretending to be Ernest.

> *On the 14th of February last. Worn out by your entire ignorance of my existence, I determined to end the matter one way or the other, and after a long struggle with myself I accepted you under this dear old tree here.*

Cecily and Algernon are a good match because, like him, Cecily's **eccentricity** means she is never dull.

Cecily is only eighteen years old, which explains her **immature** behaviour. Yet she also demonstrates **self-confidence** during her argument with the older, city-living Gwendolen.

> *This is no time for wearing the shallow mask of manners. When I see a spade I call it a spade.*

Although she is **fanciful** at times, Cecily is just as **determined** as Gwendolen and by the play's end she has achieved everything she hoped for.

Lady Bracknell

Lady Bracknell is a **matriarch** (the **strong** female head of a family). She is **bossy** and **arrogant**. She wants to **control** everyone and every situation. This is especially true when it comes to her daughter Gwendolen's marriage plans.

> *When you do become engaged to someone, I, or your father, should his health permit him, will inform you of the fact.*

Lady Bracknell sees marriage simply as an exchange of wealth and titles. She is unmoved by the idea of romance. In Act 1, she quizzes Jack to find out if he would make a proper husband for Gwendolen. When she discovers that he does not know who his parents are, she is appalled.

> *You can hardly imagine that I and Lord Bracknell would dream of allowing our only daughter—a girl brought up with the utmost care—to marry into a cloak-room, and form an alliance with a parcel?*

Likewise, in Act 3 Lady Bracknell questions Cecily's suitability to marry her nephew, Algernon. Again, Lady Bracknell shows her **avarice** (love of money) when she changes her mind about Cecily after discovering that she has a fortune.

> *A hundred and thirty thousand pounds! … Miss Cardew seems to me a most attractive young lady … We live, I regret to say, in an age of surfaces.*

Lady Bracknell's **authority** goes unchallenged until Jack outsmarts her by refusing to allow Cecily to marry Algernon unless Lady Bracknell grants him permission to marry Gwendolen.

Lady Bracknell is a **shrewd** woman, who knows exactly how to play the high-society game. She reveals that she made her way up the social ladder by sheer **determination**.

> *When I married Lord Bracknell I had no fortune of any kind. But I never dreamed for a moment of allowing that to stand in my way.*

In marrying above her social station, it is likely that Lady Bracknell came under the same **scrutiny** she now subjects others to. High society would not continue to hold so much **power** if it let people in willy-nilly. Through Lady Bracknell, Wilde satirises the **hypocrisy** of upper-class Victorian society.

Miss Prism

Although she is not one of its main characters, Cecily's governess has an important role in the play. It is Miss Prism's **careless** actions – confusing a baby with a novel – that propel the main plot: Jack's true identity.

Before her past is revealed, Miss Prism appears to uphold the Victorian ideal of **strict morality** and is **intolerant** of bad behaviour.

> *I am not in favour of this modern mania for turning bad people into good people at a moment's notice. As a man sows so let him reap.*

Yet, the fact that Miss Prism has written a novel suggests that she is not as **serious** and **strict** as she would have people believe. Popular fiction, especially written by women, was thought to be **frivolous** (silly) and improper. Furthermore, Miss Prism's more **light-hearted** side is shown when she flirts with Dr Chasuble. The two fall into each other's arms at the end of the play, suggesting that, like Jack, Miss Prism has discovered her true self.

Dr Chasuble

Like Miss Prism, Dr Chasuble allows Wilde to reflect on those who exist somewhere above servants but still well below masters on the social scale.

Dr Chasuble also professes his **strong morals** at every opportunity, yet he holds them with a more **forgiving** attitude than Miss Prism.

> *Charity, dear Miss Prism, charity! None of us are perfect.*

Chasuble considers himself a **learned** man and often uses classical references and metaphors in his speech (much to the confusion of others). He takes his position in the parish **seriously** and performs a never-ending round of christenings and sermons.

Jack and Algernon take advantage of Dr Chasuble's constant **willingness** to carry out his duties. They way they mess him around about their christenings demonstrates high society's disregard for religion, which they treat as just another way of keeping up appearances.

The **loyalty** Dr Chasuble shows to his work is also seen in his feelings for Miss Prism. When Lady Bracknell attacks Miss Prism's character in Act 3, Dr Chasuble leaps to her defence. He is rewarded with her love as the play ends.

Themes in Focus

🎭 Identity

In *The Importance of Being Earnest*, Wilde asks his audience to think about **how society defines people**. He suggests that the Victorian upper classes based their view of a person on how much money they had, the circles they moved in and especially on their **name**.

A surname indicates the **family** someone comes from. In Victorian high society, a recognisable family name or title revealed how much land a person owned, their family history and their **social prospects**. For example, the 'Lady' in Lady Augusta Bracknell immediately indicates that she is a member of the ruling classes.

By shifting the great importance that society placed on a surname to a first name, Ernest, Wilde is demonstrating just how ridiculous and **shallow** it is to judge a person simply by what they are called.

Both Jack and Algernon take on the identity of the fictional Ernest. Ernest is a 'profligate' (extravagant and immoral) young rogue.

This identity allows Jack to live a manner that is more **truthful** to who he really is. As Ernest, Jack is free to do whatever he wants, away from the responsibilities of his everyday life as Cecily's guardian in the countryside. As Ernest, his life is about the pursuit of **pleasure** and love.

> … my name is Ernest in town and Jack in the country.

Jack has always known that Worthing is not his real surname. It was given to him by Thomas Cardew 'because he happened to have a first-class ticket for Worthing in his pocket' when he found Jack as a baby. Of course, it turns out that Jack was Ernest all long. His identity as a **genuine member of high society** is confirmed and he can be fully accepted.

The Ernest identity is not that far from Algernon's real character. However, it allows him access to Jack's Manor House and to Cecily, who has been fantasising about meeting the 'wicked' Ernest for some time.

That both Cecily and Gwendolen insist on their husband being called Ernest shows how influenced women were by society's message that they must marry a man with the 'right' name. The name Ernest seems to mean more to them than the man himself. Cecily has never even met Ernest when she decides to marry him. For both women, the name symbolises good character and social standing. As Cecily says, any women who does not marry an Ernest would be poorer for it.

> I pity any poor married woman whose husband is not called Ernest.

The men's **false identities** and the women's stubbornness, of course, also leads to much confusion and provides excellent comedy.

How the characters use each other's names reveals the nature of their relationship. When they use first names, they are showing their closeness by throwing off formality. For example, when Cecily and Gwendolen first meet in Act 2 they insist on using each other's first names.

> *I may call you Cecily, may I not?*

But when the women argue, they return to calling each other Miss Cardew and Miss Fairfax.

> *I warn you, Miss Cardew, you may go too far.*

Wilde also uses names to provide **clues** about his characters. A 'chasuble' is an item of clothing worn by the clergy, telling us that much of Dr Chasuble's identity comes from his role in the church. The name 'Prism' is close to the word 'prim', which means disapproving of bad behaviour. Lady Bracknell's first name, Augusta, tells us that she is an 'august' person – someone who commands respect.

Love and Marriage

As well as being a major aspect of the plot, marriage is often discussed by the play's characters. In Act 1, when Jack tells Algernon that he has come to London to propose to Gwendolen, Algernon says:

> *I thought you had come up for pleasure? . . . I call that business.*

In Victorian high society, marriage was thought of as a **social duty** rather than an expression of love. As Algernon explains:

> *It is very romantic to be in love. But there is nothing romantic about a definite proposal.*

A good match was the best way to protect or elevate a family's position in society. Lady Bracknell represents this way of thinking exactly. As the head of her family, it is Lady Bracknell's responsibility to assess the **suitability** of anyone wishing to marry one of her relatives.

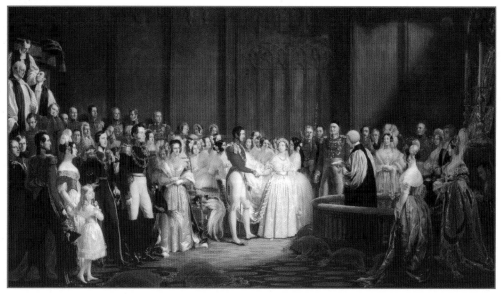

Queen Victoria's wedding

In Act 1, Lady Bracknell interviews Jack to see if he would make a good husband for her daughter. She is delighted to hear of Jack's **wealth**. However, she is disgusted when she discovers that Jack was found in a handbag in the cloakroom of a train station, as this means Jack does not have a clear family ancestry.

> *You can hardly imagine that I and Lord Bracknell would dream of allowing our only daughter—a girl brought up with the utmost care—to marry into a cloak-room, and form an alliance with a parcel? Good morning, Mr Worthing!*

At the end of the play, it is revealed that Gwendolen and Jack are cousins. However, the other characters do not comment on this because cousins commonly married in the Victorian age in order to maintain a family's wealth and social position. In fact, Queen Victoria married her first cousin, Prince Albert.

During the **social season**, wealthy women of marriageable age were taken to parties and balls, where they could meet **eligible** men. However, the choice of husband was rarely left to them, as Lady Bracknell explains when she finds out that Gwendolen has accepted Jack's proposal:

> *An engagement should come on a young girl as a surprise, pleasant or unpleasant, as the case may be. It is hardly a matter that she could be allowed to arrange for herself …*

A Victorian cartoon about the social season

In Act 3, Lady Bracknell questions Cecily's **worthiness** to marry her nephew, Algernon. Again, she is impressed when she discovers that Cecily has a large fortune. Once more, Wilde reminds his audience that marriage is largely seen as a purely **financial transaction**.

However, the younger characters in the play do question this **custom**. Jack, Algernon, Gwendolen and Cecily all sincerely love their partners. When Lady Bracknell praises the 'distinct social possibilities in Miss Cardew's profile', Algernon says that he doesn't care what society thinks because he truly loves Cecily.

> *Cecily is the sweetest, dearest, prettiest girl in the whole world. And I don't care twopence about social possibilities.*

Love gives some much needed likeability to the central characters. Although Wilde is **attacking the traditions of Victorian marriage**, he **champions love** as a quality that is beyond corruption. As the curtain falls, all the main characters are **happily paired**; even Miss Prism and Dr Chasuble fall into a loving embrace.

Social Class

As a **comedy of manners**, *The Importance of Being Earnest* portrays **stereotypical** posh characters and shows them acting foolishly in order to satirise the entire **gentry**. Throughout the play, Wilde questions the values of upper-class Victorian society.

The play opens on Algernon, an indulgent, wealthy gentleman surrounded in luxury. It is not long before he is joined by his friend Jack and we learn that both men spend much of their time telling lies and gallivanting around the country. As Algernon says:

> *My duty as a gentleman has never interfered with my pleasures in the smallest degree.*

Members of high society, Wilde suggests, have so little of importance to occupy them that they do nothing but get into trivial 'scrapes'. Thus raising the question: are the ruling classes worthy of the respect they demand?

Lady Bracknell is a self-appointed gatekeeper of **upper-class values**. Maintaining the family wealth and name is of the utmost importance to her. She dreads any change in the **status quo** (social order) that might see the lower classes rise up, and fears 'revolutionary outrage' taking place in England. Unsurprisingly, Lady Bracknell has the greatest regard for a tradition that puts her at the top of the pecking order:

> *Never speak disrespectfully of Society, Algernon. Only people who can't get into it do that.*

Even the play's **middle-class** characters obey the **rigid class system**. In Act 2, Miss Prism scolds Cecily for watering the flowers as that is a job for a lower-ranking person:

> *Cecily, Cecily! Surely such a utilitarian occupation as the watering of flowers is rather Moulton's duty than yours?*

Although she ranks far lower than the play's main characters, Miss Prism enjoys being superior to those even lower down the social scale. She reveals that she has 'often spoken to the poorer classes on the subject' of how many children they have.

The **servant class** in the play are shown going about their duties carefully and without fuss. Their steady behaviour highlights their masters' recklessness by contrast.

👄 Secrets and Lies

In *The Importance of Being Earnest*, Wilde shows a society that rewards those who keep secrets and tell lies. As long as there is an appearance of **propriety** (good manners), the truth does not matter. Gwendolen perfectly sums up this attitude when she says:

> *In matters of grave importance, style, not sincerity is the vital thing.*

Both Jack and Algernon are happy to live **double lives**. By pretending to be Ernest, the men are failing to be **earnest** (sincere and serious). Algernon calls this lifestyle Bunburying, which suggests he sees **deception** as little more than a **game**.

The Victorians are known for their **strict morals**. Yet, Wilde portrays a world in which most people secretly enjoy **immorality**. When Cecily first meets Algernon, whom she believes to be the famously wicked Ernest, she tells him:

> *I hope you have not been leading a double life, pretending to be wicked and being really good all the time.*

Miss Prism prides herself on her good morals, yet she is keeping a huge secret: that she lost a baby because she was too absorbed with writing her novel. It is this **revelation** that brings the play to its conclusion.

While they come under mild fire from Gwendolen and Cecily when their lies are exposed, in the end Jack and Algernon win the women's hands in marriage. Indeed, despite the **tricks** they have played, their love for the women seems **sincere**. Yet, although the play's title and final line suggest that it is important to be earnest, the plot that has gone before suggests that sincerity is not always necessary to succeed in a society that values appearance above all else.

Approaching Exam Questions

When you come to prepare for exam questions, you should keep the following checklist in mind.

☑ Analyse, Create, Edit (ACE)

In all tasks, it is important that you **analyse** what work you are required to do, **create** that work to the best of your ability and then **review and edit** what you have done. See **page 155** for a step-by-step guide to using ACE to answer an examination question.

Always take the time to read the question properly and figure out what exactly what you are being asked to do.

☑ Write Effective Paragraphs

At the heart of any good written answer is well-made paragraphs. When you are completing written tasks, make sure that each paragraphs shows:

- A confident opinion (include a **topic sentence** that expresses the main idea).
- Evidence of how your opinion was formed (supporting quotes and references).
- A clear structure (engaging opening and conclusion).
- A fully developed idea/point.
- Varied and relevant language.
- Good spelling and grammar.

☑ Read

The best way to improve your language range is to read as much as possible. Having the right word can really bring an answer together and make it clear what you are trying to say. Try to keep your sentences short and to the point.

You can record any new words you encounter while reading *The Importance of Being Earnest* on **page 77** of your portfolio. Your teacher will guide you in the correct use of a word.

☑ Revise

Reread the play before your exam. Make revision notes about the following features:

- Main characters
- Key events
- Important quotes
- Central themes
- Literary devices/terms
- Staging.

Answering a Question About Theme in *The Importance of Being Earnest*

Question: From a dramatic text you have studied, explain how the dramatist developed a particular theme or issue.

Analyse (Plan)

1. First, choose which theme to discuss. As part of your study of *The Importance of Being Earnest* you will have considered four central themes:

   - Identity
   - Love and marriage
   - Social class
   - Secrets and lies.

   You may also have considered other themes with your teacher.

2. The question asks 'how the dramatist developed' the theme or issue. Think about:
   - Plot (key events that relate to your chosen theme)
   - Characters (what they say and do that relates to your chosen theme)
   - Use of motif and symbols.

3. Create a brief outline of your answer to make sure you are answering the question and that you are clear about the sequence of your ideas. For example, if you chose identity as your theme, your outline might look as follows:

Theme:
Identity

Introduction:
Explain how Wilde introduced the theme and developed it over the course of the play. Wilde asks his audience to consider how important a name (the symbol of a person's identity) really is. He does this in a number of ways.

Paragraph 1:
Plot. State that the whole plot of the play centers on false identities. Jack and Algernon pretend to be Ernest in order to have fun and find love (Bunburying). Jack doesn't know who he really is because he was found as a baby after being lost by Miss Prism. In the end, it turns out that Jack is truly called Ernest and is a member of the upper class.

Paragraph 2:
Characters. What someone is called, where they come from and what family they were born into is all important to the play's upper-class Victorian characters. Cecily and Gwendolen insist that their husband is called Ernest. Cecily says that she could not give Algernon her 'undivided attention' if he had any other name. Lady Bracknell questions Jack and Cecily to decide if they are good enough to marry into her family.

Paragraph 3:
Motif. Wilde uses the motif of names throughout (Ernest, meanings of character names, lists of names). How characters address each other tells us about their relationship (Cecily and Gwendolen tea table argument).

Conclusion:
Through plot, characterisation and motif, Wilde explores the theme of identity to show just how shallow it is to judge a person simply by what they are called. In this way, *The Importance of Being Earnest* criticises a Victorian society that does not look beneath the surface.

Note: While it is essential that you plan your answer carefully, you must make sure that you leave yourself enough **time** to write the answer. Consider how much time you have for each question. Sometimes, if you have not had time to finish your answer, the examiner will look over your plan to see if they can give you extra marks.

Create

1. Introduction

- Show that you have read and **understand the question**. This question asks **how** a theme was developed by the dramatist. **Focus** on this approach, rather than simply writing everything you know about your chosen theme.

- Your introduction should also give a **brief summary** of the shape your answer will take. Rather than listing the points you are going to make, introduce the ideas you feel are most important in answering the question in a general way.

2. Paragraphs

- Keep in mind the check list on writing effective paragraphs on **page 154**.

- Building an argument. Paragraphs do not have to be completely separate points. You can reference something you have already mentioned or will look at in more detail later in your answer.

3. Conclusion

- Do not simply repeat the points you have already made in the main part of the answer. Your conclusion should **reflect** on what you have said in your essay. It is an overall, broader version of your argument.

- Have your conclusion in mind before you begin writing your answer. Creating a brief outline before you start, as shown on **page 155**, will help. Knowing where your answer is going will keep you focused as you write.

Edit

1. Before

- Look over your outline. If any of your initial ideas do not answer the question, leave them out of your answer.

2. During

- As you write, remain alert to any ideas that are not answering the question. Refer back to the question and ask yourself if you are answering it.

- Try to write as clearly and correctly as possible, so that there are fewer errors to spot and correct when you have finished.

3. After

- If you are completing a question for homework you have plenty of time to read back over your work. Correct any spelling and grammatical errors and add extra points if necessary.

- In an exam situation, always **leave enough time to read over your work at least once**.

The ACE Balance

Each part of ACE supports the others:

- If you do not **analyse** before you **create**, you will have to **edit** more than someone who has planned their answer.
- If you have taken too much time to **analyse** a question, you may not be have enough time to **create** and **edit** your answer as you would have hoped.

The following time guide is useful:

- Analyse for 15 per cent of the time.
- Create for 75 per cent of the time.
- Edit for 10 per cent of the time.

For example, if you have 20 minutes to answer a question:

- Analyse for 3 minutes.
- Create for 15 minutes.
- Edit for 2 minutes.

Over time, you will develop a sense of how to make ACE work best for you and for the question you are answering. Your teacher will give you feedback on which part of the ACE process you need to work on to improve the standard of your work.

CREATION   TIME